LOVED AND LOVING

LOVED AND LOVING

Contemplation to Attain God's Love

Jacqueline Syrup Bergan and Marie Schwan, CSJ

ISBN: 197624143X
ISBN 13: 9781976241437

IN CELEBRATION OF MARIE'S LIFE AND WORK

MARIE SCHWAN, CSJ
1933-2014

ALL FOR THE HONOR AND GLORY OF GOD

Cover Design

See how they love each other.

—JOHN 13:34–35

As we look at the image of the lovely sheep with their serene faces and long eyelashes, our awareness is quickened in the realization that they are, indeed, loved and being loving. As all authentic art does, Gregg Rochester's art moves the psyche/soul from the images portrayed to a mirroring of a profound transcendent reality. His depiction of the actions of the five sheep beautifully renders the invisible energy and silent ecstasy of the love that moves between them. Looking deeply, we see the tender sweetness of love, the expansion of compassion and healing; we intuit the emergent wholeness of community created by the self-giving loving of the sheep.

Having been artistically represented in the mosaic art of basilicas and sarcophagus throughout the centuries, the use of the symbol of sheep has a profound significance. Among Greeks and Romans, as well as other cultures, sheep were seen as depictions of Gods or Goddesses or as a fitting sacrifice to placate the Gods, to demonstrate their faith and obedience in order to obtain highly prized favors from God.

The symbolism of sheep is an important part of our Christian tradition. Jesus has been given the title of the Lamb of God; his death on the cross to atone for sins is analogous to a sacrificial lamb depicted in the earlier centuries.

Our contemporary theologians, however, are gifting us with a fuller meaning of Christ's death. Ilia Delio teaches us, "We have failed to see the wisdom of the cross when we have assimilated and fostered, in a distorted way, an emphasis of sin over love as if, the primary meaning of the death of Jesus is a punishment willed by the father to make up for and save us from our sins". (Delio, 2005, 52–53).

Jesus is also frequently referred to as a shepherd or sheep and his followers as his flock. The church of today is being led to embrace this symbolism of love and protection over and above that of atonement. We are seeking, as an evolving Christian community, to interrupt the death of Christ as a kenotic expression of love, a self-emptying love of the world and the cosmos, rather than as a ransom payment.

The image of sheep as a symbol for Christ and his followers serves as a perfect inspiration for this new paradigm of a loving community. This community of love could be referred to as Teilhard de Chardin's Christogenesis, the process of becoming the image of Christ in the world, "the growth of the ever greater Christ". (de Chardin, 133).

Beatrice Bruteau speaks of this community of love as all creation participating in "a sharing in the creative act of God's ecstasy which is kin to the kenosis of self-emptying love of Phillippians 2:6—God empties Godself—it is the defining divine act: self-giving, being-bestowing. Ecstasy has the connotations of extreme love and supreme joy". (Bruteau, (997, 998).

And so we move back to Rochester's dynamic image of our loved and loving sheep. We see them in their innocence, simplicity, and gentle tenderness of love. We are aware of how they totally lay down their lives: giving flesh to the strong, milk to the weak, and fleece to the cold.

We see them, and we love them.

Contents

Forward

Who, in his or her spiritual journey, has not wished to live in "the Divine Milieu," and be inundated with the sense of the Presence of God everywhere and at all times? I mean a loving Divine Presence in our personal friendships and relationships, in our contact with the created world, as well as in our joys and sufferings, our successes and failures, even in our sinfulness.

In writing *Loved and Loving: Contemplation to Attain God's Love*, Jacqueline Syrup Bergan and Marie Schwan, CSJ, have collaborated to make this wish come true. As before, with their acclaimed five-volume work, *Take and Receive*, they use the spiritual exercises of St. Ignatius of Loyola to help us achieve a strong sense of the Presence of God, a God of great and encompassing love, always and everywhere.

"God bends low in love." In this beautiful expression, the authors assert that God's presence and closeness to us comes through Jesus, the Christ, God's Son, God's word, who became flesh and lived among us. And so as they say, "It's all about Jesus."

It's about his interior life of deep communion with his Father and praying to his Father, by which we see that the Father and the

Son are "in love" with each other, a love so intense, so enrapturing, that this love gives rise to and is personified in the Holy Spirit. The authors note that this interior life of our Triune God enables us to profess God as Lover, Loved, and Loving.

Our life of prayer, in fact, our whole life, is "all about Jesus," not only in his Trinitarian relationships, but also it's in his compassionate way of loving the lowly and selflessly serving others unto death and into resurrection.

When we contemplate Jesus, "who is in the bosom of the Father," (John 1, 18 RSV) and when we meditate on and/or contemplate the saving events of his life, then we, enlightened by the Holy Spirit, Gift of God to us, come to understand, as the authors so beautifully put it, that, "When God's love spilled over into creation, God thought of me," so that "I am from love, of love, and for love."

Born of God, who is Love, we are daughters and sons of God, called to love God with all our heart and mind, and soul. And so we are sisters and brothers, called to love one another as Jesus loved us all.

I am convinced that this work by Jacqueline and Marie will deepen our love relationship with our Triune God and with each other. Then we would enter ever more deeply into the "Divine Milieu."

Bishop Victor H. Balke, Bishop-emeritus of Crookston (MN.)

Acknowledgements

I wish to acknowledge and express gratitude to all those who have supported, affirmed, and encouraged Marie and me through nearly forty years of ministry.

Throughout the years, Dick Rice and Christina Wright personally mentored us in wisdom and grace.

In the early years of our ministry Marie and I gave numerous retreats and days of prayer in the parishes of the Diocese of Crookston. I extend gratitude to the people and priests of the Diocese who warmly welcomed us and supported us in our endeavor to bring the love of scripture, as it is expressed in the Exercises of St. Ignatius of Loyola, to their parishes.

*I especially thank Bishop Victor Balke who extended to us the warmth of friendship, support, and affirmation. He consistently encouraged our writing and wrote the Forward in our first guide for prayer, **Love**, and now graciously has written the Forward in, this our last work, **Loved and Loving**.*

And to Marie's sisters, the Sisters of St. Joseph, I extend immense gratitude.

They supported us in every possible way; giving us space in the convent to write, hours of secretarial help, and, even, one Lenten season, baking several hundred hot cross buns for us to distribute in a special ritual to retreatants throughout the diocese. Their greatest contribution to our ministry was, of course, their unfailing, emotional support.

I am deeply grateful to my family; my husband Leonard, my three sons- John Lanz, Thomas Lanz and James Lanz, and my stepdaughter, Stacy Rusling. They supported me in so many ways, especially being patient with me when I spent long hours in study, writing, and for the times I was absent giving retreats and workshops. Without their love and support, my ministry would not have been possible.

My daughter-in-law, Wendy Beaton-Lanz, deserves a huge thank you. She is responsible for the beautiful , creative lay out of the cover, spine and back cover of Loved and Loving.

To our publishers I extend a debt of gratitude for their belief and confidence in our ministry.

I recognize our readers for their on-going love and support and am grateful to those who have used our books in their ministry, adapting them to their own voice, to further the work of Ignatius.

A large measure of appreciation goes to the artists who have graced our books with their exquisite creativity - Donna Pierce Campbell for her beautiful birds that embraced the five volume **Take and Receive** series, and Gregg Rochester whose enchanting sheep, I know, will serve to invite many into **Loved and Loving**.

Marie and I were never alone…

> Always present was the spirit of Ignatius of Loyola, gracing us with abundant guidance.

> The spirit of the risen Christ gifted us with inspiration and empowerment.

Our hearts were deeply touched by all the love and support we received.

In gratitude, Jacqueline

Introduction

PART I

The age of compassion is here. We, as people of the world, God's people, are being gathered together in an accelerated movement of the Spirit that is characterized by mercy and joy, forgiveness, and repentance. This gathering is palpable in the ever-increasing level of awareness that we are all one people, one humanity born of God's creative love. It is not so unlike the feminine image we are given in the Gospel of Matthew (23:37) of the mother hen who calls her scattered chicks to gather around her, clucking at them in a low tone, sometimes tucking them under her wing, not for protection only but for the gathering together of her family (Lohfink 2012, 63).

The heightened sense of being one, of being "family," with the world community is undeniable. Every day, our technologically advanced media makes alarmingly visible to us the incredible sufferings of people throughout the world. It is in our personal heart-wrenching experience of deep sadness for the dispersed, broken, and despairing that, at last, we see them as brothers and sisters.

We are being graced by God with a new heart and a new spirit. The hardness of our hearts is being removed, and we are being given hearts of compassion (Ezek. 36:26). A new thing is happening; it is as if we are being brought home. Yet, the promise has always been here and our home, too, always present within us. In spite of distractions and regressions, there has been a constant leaning forward to the "more." At this moment in history, God is sending forth a surge of grace manifested as a call to compassion and mercy. Paradoxically, it is through the pain of dissolution that God's promise is coming to fruition (Ezekiel 64ff). It seems it is always that way. Slowly, through history, we move forward ever more deeply into oneness with God and each other.

Pope Francis leads us to look at the story of the call of Matthew: "Jesus saw a publican, and since he looked at him with feelings of love and chose him, he said to him, 'Follow me'" (Pope Francis 2013, 16). Even though we, too, are burdened with the innate weakness of the human condition, Jesus looks at each of us with love and mercy and invites us to participate in his great work. In looking at us with eyes of love, he empowers us to look at others with that same empowering love. The call is to see the world with the eyes of Jesus, to look deeply, to participate in his work of healing the wounded (*Lumen Fidei*, para. 18).

How do we go about "seeing with the eyes of Jesus"? Pope Francis sends us to St. Paul for a description of the manner of living that is required if we are to live with the intensity and commitment of faith that enables us to share in Jesus's way of seeing. We must believe and live as children of God.

Everyone moved by the spirit is a son [and daughter] of God. The spirit you received is not the spirit of slaves bringing fear into your lives again: it is the spirit of sons and daughters, and makes us cry out, "Abba Father." (Rom. 8:14–16)

In accepting the gift of faith, believers become a new creation; they receive new being; as God's children, they are now "sons in the Son." The phrase "Abba Father," so characteristic of Jesus' own experience, now becomes the core of the Christian experience. The core of faith, as a filial existence, is the acknowledgement of a primordial and radical gift which upholds our lives...Only by being open to and acknowledging this gift can we be transformed, experience salvation and bear good fruit. (*Lumen Fidei*, para. 19).

This new way of seeing things is centered on Christ. It follows, then, that if we are to authentically respond to his call, we must draw near to him. We must become, in the way of Ignatius of Loyola, "contemplatives in action." Through a faithful daily practice of praying with scripture, we learn Christ's way of seeing and healing and we become one with his spirit.

In calling us to be bearers of compassion, Pope Francis has shared with us his dream:

I dream of a church that is a mother and shepherdess. The church's ministers must be merciful, take responsibility for people and accompany them like the good Samaritan who washes, cleans and raises up his neighbor...The ministers of the gospel must be people who can warm the hearts of the people, who walk through the dark night with them, who know how to dialogue and to descend themselves into their people's night, into the darkness, but without getting lost. (Pope Francis 2013, 24)

He continues by saying that this can happen only if there is a contemplative attitude. The signs that one is on the right path are "profound peace, spiritual consolation, love of God and love of all things in God" (Pope Francis., 30).

A life lived in compassionate service is our grateful response for the gifts of God's extravagant love and his continuing laboring on our behalf.

PART II

At the end of the *Spiritual Exercises*, authored by St. Ignatius of Loyola in the sixteenth century, there is an exercise that has come to be known simply as "the Contemplatio." The exercise has two pre-notes describing love as a mutual gifting and more present in deeds than in words. This is followed by a fourfold contemplation of the gifts of God, and the human response held in the thrust of the Suscipe, a prayer of offering beginning with "Take, Lord, receive all..."

In the first point, the retreatant is invited to contemplate the mystery that God gives and brings to memory the many gifts of God, gifts of life, family, opportunities, and so on.

In the second point, the retreatant, deepens the awareness that God inhabits all creatures, giving them being, coming to us as a sacrament, making of us a dwelling place.

In the third point, the retreatant considers how God labors-for me-like a mother giving birth, like a potter, a bread maker, a farmer.

Finally, with an awareness of God as both giver and gift, lavishing love upon me, like the sun pouring down its life-giving light and warmth and energy, God descends.

Given the mutuality of love, each movement of God elicits a response. As St. Ignatius says, if I am to give a reasonable response, I will pray the prayer,

> Take, Lord, and receive, all my liberty, my memory, my understanding, and my entire will—all that I have and call my own. You have given it all to me. To you, Lord, I return it. Everything is yours, do with it what you will. Give me only your love and your grace. That is enough for me.

Retreat directors have frequently puzzled about how to use this exercise. Is it the climax of the Exercises or simply an important way of praying? Is it a highly condensed form of the kernel of the Exercises? Is it to be divided into four prayer periods on a single day, or incorporated into the fourth week, and so on?

In recent years, there has been a growing awareness that this Exercise was initially given by Ignatius, to the novices who were returning home after having come to Rome as pilgrims to make the month-long Spiritual Exercises. At the end of this incredible spiritual experience, they were eager to return to their various homelands to begin to "co-labor with Jesus." Ignatius knew that by the end of their long retreat, they were men in love with Jesus Christ and his mission. He gave them as their prayer for the journey home what has come to be known as the Contemplatio.

Ignatius told them to keep their eyes and their hearts open, for as men in love they would see what they had never really seen before—the majesty of the mountains, the strength of the winds, the beauty of the flowers, and so on. These, he told them, they would now see as God's gifts to them. What would be their response? *Take Lord, receive...*

Not only would they see the mountains and trees and flowers as God's gifts to them, but they would experience *in* the majesty of the mountains, the majesty of God, and in the strength of the winds, the strength of God, and so on.

As they experienced the seasonal changes and the people at work in the fields, they would become more aware of how God labored in and for them, and finally they would be overwhelmed how all these gifts were showered on them like rain, or like the beams of sunlight.

So the journey home would be a pilgrimage, and the contemplation that marked the journey would become a way of life for the rest of their lives. Scholars suggest that everything that follows the Spiritual Exercises in the Society of Jesus is an expression of the Contemplatio.

The Contemplatio is the crown and fruit of the Exercises. It is a way of life.

It is as a "way of life" that we have approached the writing of this book, with the desire to make available to those who make use of it, the deepening of the grace that was Ignatius's own and which was described in the words of one of his early companions, Fr. Nadal:

> I shall not fail to recall that grace which Ignatius had in all circumstance while at work or in conversation, of feeling the presence of God and of tasting spiritual things, of being contemplative even in the midst of action; he used to interpret this as seeking God in all things.

"Thanks be to God, who…through us is spreading everywhere the fragrance of the knowledge of himself. To God we are the fragrance of Christ both among those who are being saved…the smell of life leading to life" (2 Cor 2:14–16).

Orientations

Luke 11:1

Lord, teach us to pray.

Prayer is our personal response to God's presence. We approach the Lord reverently with a listening heart. God speaks first. In prayer, we acknowledge the Divine presence and in gratitude respond to God in love. The focus is always on God and on what God does.

The following suggestions are offered as ways of supporting and enabling attentiveness to God's word and awareness of our unique response.

A. Daily Pattern of Prayer

For each period of prayer, use the following pattern:

1. Preparation
    — Plan to spend at least twenty minutes to one hour in prayer daily. Though there is nothing sacred about sixty minutes, most people find that an hour better provides

for the quieting of self, the entrance into the passage, and so on.

— The evening before, take time to read the commentary as well as the scriptural passage for the following day. Just before falling asleep, recall the scripture passage.

2. Structure of the Prayer Period

— Quiet yourself; be still inside and out. Relax. Breathe in deeply, hold your breath to the count of four, and then exhale slowly through your mouth. Repeat several times.

— Realize you are nothing without God; declare your dependency.

— Ask God for the grace you want and need.

— Read and reflect on your chosen scriptural passage, using the appropriate form; for example, use meditation for poetic and nonstory passages, Ignatian contemplation for story-event passages, and so on. See "Forms of Solitary Prayer,"

— Spend the last fifteen to twenty minutes in contemplative prayer.

— Close the prayer period with a time of conversation with Jesus and his Father. Speak and listen. Conclude with an Our Father.

3. Review of Prayer

The review of prayer is a reflection at the conclusion of the prayer period. The purpose of the review is to heighten our awareness of how God has been present to us during the prayer period.

The review focuses primarily on the interior movements of consolation and desolation as they are revealed in our feelings of joy, peace, sadness, fear, ambivalence, anger. Often it is in the review that we become aware of how God has responded to our request for a particular grace.

Writing the review provides for personal accountability and is a precious record of our spiritual journey. To write the review is a step toward self-integration. In the absence of a spiritual director or a spiritual companion, the writing helps fill the need for evaluation and clarification. If one has a spiritual director, the written review offers an excellent means of preparing to share one's prayer experience.

Method: In a notebook or journal, after each prayer period, indicate the date and the passage. Answer each of the following questions:

— Did any word or phrase particularly strike you?
— What were your feelings: Were you peaceful? loving? trusting? sad? discouraged? What do these feelings say to you?
— How are you more aware of God's presence?
— Would returning to some point be helpful in your next prayer period?

B. Forms of Solitary Prayer

Scriptural prayer has various forms, and different forms appeal to different people. Eventually, by trying various methods, we become adept at using approaches that are appropriate to particular passages and are in harmony with our personality and needs.

One can consider that each form and practice is a portal into the presence of God.

This guide will make use of the following forms:

1. Meditation

In meditation, we approach the scripture passage like a love letter; this approach is especially helpful in praying poetic passages. It may be used, also, in pondering a prayer, like the Our Father, or another prayer from our rich Christian tradition.

Method:

— Read the passage slowly, aloud or in a whisper, letting the words wash over you.
— Stay with the words that especially catch your attention; savor them; absorb them the way the thirsty earth receives the rain.
— Keep repeating the word or phrase, aware of the feelings and memories that are awakened.
— Read and reread the passage lovingly as you would a letter from a dear friend, or as you would softly sing the chorus of a song.

2. Ignatian Contemplation

In Ignatian contemplation, we enter into a life event or story passage of the scriptures by way of imagination, making use of all our senses. One puts aside one's critical, analytical mind.

Theologians tell us that through contemplation we are able to "recall and be present at the mysteries of Christ's life" (English 1995, 149). We meet the Risen Christ in the living memories that form the Gospel.

The Spirit of Jesus, present within us through Baptism, teaches us, just as Jesus taught the Apostles. The Spirit recalls and enlivens the particular mystery into which we enter through prayer. Just as in the Eucharist the Risen Christ makes present the paschal mystery, in this prayer he brings forward the particular event we are contemplating and presents himself within the mystery.

Method: In contemplation, we enter the story as if we are there.

— Watch what happens; listen to what is being said.
— Bring all your senses to life as you enter into the scene: what you see, hear, smell, and so on.
— Become part of the mystery; closely observe what is happening, or assume the role of one of the persons.
— Look at one of the individuals; what does he or she experience? How does he or she interact with others?
— What difference does it make for my life, my family, for society, if I hear the message?

In the Gospel stories, enter into dialogue with Jesus.

— Be there with him and for him.
— Want him; hunger for him.
— Listen to him.
— Respond to him (Veltri 1998, 5-6).

3. Lectio Divina

"Listen to the words I say. Open your mouth and eat what I am about to give you. Eat this scroll...And Ezekiel says, 'I ate it, and it tasted sweet as honey'" (Ezek. 2:8, 3:3).

There is an ancient monastic practice for praying scripture known as *lectio divina*, Latin for "sacred reading." There are four phases or moments to this form of prayer. In Latin, they rhyme: *lectio* or reading; *meditatio*, meditation; *oratio*, prayer; and *contemplatio*, contemplation.

One begins the prayer period with *lectio*, that is, the reading of a verse or short passage of scripture. The words are read over and over in a prayerful way, in a whisper, or aloud if one is alone. With each reading, a different word can be emphasized. For example, "*My* shepherd is the Lord...My *shepherd* is the Lord...My shepherd *is* the Lord...My shepherd is *the Lord.*" *Lectio* is a way of reading that is also deep listening. Its purpose is not to gain knowledge but to deeply taste the Word of God.

Lectio flows into *meditatio* or meditation. Here one uses the mind to think about the passage. What do I know of shepherds and of sheep? What have been my experiences, even vicariously, with sheep and shepherds, images I have seen, and so on? Who or what in my life is "the Lord"? Do I look to God as my leader, guide, source of hope, and so on?

Reflecting on the images and experiences that are awakened within me through this passage, I enter into *oratio*, addressing to

God my spontaneous petitions, thanksgiving, acts of adoration and of praise and of sorrow. "My God, truly I want you to be my shepherd, to lead and protect me, and to lead me out of danger. I ask for forgiveness for the many times that I have been unfaithful. I thank you for how you continue to call me even when I am most lost and entangled, and so on."

If at any moment in the *lectio, meditation, oratio,* I find myself interiorly moved by a sense of peace, joy, loving sorrow, hope, or any other feeling, I allow myself to be very quiet, entering into the stillness of *contemplatio,* simply resting in the presence of God.

This approach to scriptural prayer is a whole-person approach. The body is engaged in the initial reading, the mind in the reflection, the will in the spontaneous prayer, and the heart in the contemplative silence.

A Benedictine Sister, long practiced in the use of lectio for her prayer, suggested that the four-part prayer is completed in *compassio,* that is, in compassion, the overflowing of God's love and care in service.

4. Centering Prayer

Be still and know that I am God.

Centering Prayer is a way of praying that can facilitate contemplation and lead to an interior transformation. For a more in-depth explanation of Centering Prayer, see Appendix B.

Father Keating suggests that one set aside twenty minutes, twice a day for centering prayer. The method is as follows:

(1) Choose a sacred word, such as "Lord," or "Abba," or "Jesus," or "let go."
(2) Sit comfortably with eyes closed, and silently introduce the sacred word "inwardly and gently as if laying a feather on a piece of absorbent cotton."
(3) When any thoughts, feelings, images, memories, and so on surface, gently return to the sacred word.
(4) At the end of the prayer period, remain quiet for several minutes, then gently and slowly pray the Our Father (adapted from "Father Thomas Keating Brings Contemplation Out of the Cloister," 13).

5. Meditative Reading

"I opened my mouth; he gave me the scroll to eat and then said, '…feed on this scroll which I am giving you and eat your fill.' So I ate it, and it tasted sweet as honey" (Ezek. 3:2–3).

One of the approaches to prayer is a reflective reading of the scriptures or other spiritual writings.

Spiritual reading is always enriching to our life of prayer. The method described below is especially supportive in times when prayer is difficult or dry.

Method: Read slowly, pausing periodically to allow the words and phrases to enter into you. When a thought resonates deeply, stay with it, allowing the fullness of it to penetrate your being. Relish the word received. Respond authentically and spontaneously, as in a dialogue.

6. Poetry as Prayer

Through poetry, we are frequently drawn into an -"aha"- moment of grace and insight. In his book, *Poetry as Prayer*, Robert Waldron says:

> Through the poetic experience we come to experience the deeper, fuller, richer possibility of life and are confronted with the folly of our superficiality and self centeredness. We are insistently and powerfully beckoned by true poetry to live more fully in the light and vibrancy of Reality. This demands a dying to the false self...and a courageous entering into the wondrous realms of the true self, the self that is the image of God, of Divine Beauty, ever coming forth from God's inexhaustible creative love.

Waldron suggest the following ten steps as a way of approaching a poem:

(1) Choose a poem to pray. It need not be a religious poem.
(2) Choose a quiet place where you can be alone with the poem.
(3) Read the poem aloud.
(4) Focus your attention completely on the poem.
(5) If you feel so moved, look up definitions of the words you don't understand, but do not be obsessive about complete comprehension.

(6) Note the capitalization and punctuation which may be clues to the deeper meaning of the poem.

(7) Attention to poetic figures of speech, such as metaphor, simile, alliteration, etc., may open your insight into the various layers of meaning.

(8) After sitting quietly, reread the poem.

(9) Do not be concerned if you feel you have not grasped the meaning of the poem; trust that the effort of your attention is never wasted.

(10) Consider memorizing the poem so that it is always available to you, to calm or to inspire you. (Waldron 123–25)

7. Welcoming Prayer, See Appendix B.

8. Journaling

"A reading of [my words] will enable you to perceive my understanding of the mystery of Christ" (Eph. 3:4).

Journaling is meditative writing. When we place pen on paper, spirit and body cooperate to release our true selves.

There is a difference between journaling and keeping a journal.

To journal is to experience ourselves in a new light as expression is given to the fresh images that emerge from our subconscious. Journaling requires putting aside preconceived ideas and control.

Meditative writing is like writing a letter to one we love. We recall memories, clarify convictions, and our affections well up within us. In writing we may discover that emotions are intensified and prolonged.

Because of this, journaling can also serve in identifying and healing hidden, suppressed emotions such as anger, fear, and resentment.

Finally, journaling can give one a deeper appreciation for the written words we encounter in scripture.

Method: Among the many variations of journaling as prayer are the following:

— writing a letter addressed to God. Writing a conversation between oneself and Jesus. The dialogue can also be with an event, an experience, or a value. It is possible to dialogue with a death or separation, or wisdom. One gives them personal attributes and imagines them as person with whom one enters into conversation.
— writing an answer to a question, such as "What do you want me to do for you?" (Mark 10:51), or "Why are you weeping?" (John 20:15).
— allowing Jesus or another person from scripture to speak to us through the writing.

9. Repetition

"I will remain quietly meditating upon the point in which I have found what I desire without any eagerness to go on till I have been satisfied." (St. Ignatius of Loyola, Veltri 1998, vol. 1, 110)

Repetition is the return to a precious period of prayer for the purpose of allowing the movements of God to deepen within one's heart.

Through repetitions, we fine-tune our sensitivities to God and to how God speaks in our prayer and within our life circumstances. The prayer of repetition allows for the experience of integrating who we are with who God is revealing himself to be for us.

Repetition is a way of honoring God's word to us in the earlier prayer period. It is recalling and pondering an earlier conversation with one we love. It is as if we say to God, "Tell me that again; what did I hear you saying?"

In this follow-up conversation, or repetition, we open ourselves to a healing presence that often transforms whatever sadness and confusion we may have experienced in the first prayer.

In repetitions, not only is our consolation (joy, warmth, peace) deepened but our desolation (pain, sadness, confusion) is frequently better understood and accepted within God's plan for us.

Method: The period of prayer that we select to repeat is one in which we have experienced a significant movement of joy or sadness or confusion. It may also be a period in which nothing seemed to happen, due, perhaps, to our own lack of readiness at the time.

— Recall the feelings of the first period of prayer.
— As a point of entry, use the scene, word, or feeling that was previously most significant.
— Allow the spirit to direct the inner movements of your heart during this time of prayer.

Spiritual Practices and Helps

1. Examen of Consciousness

"Yahweh, you examine me and know me" (Ps. 139:1).

The examen of consciousness, sometimes called an awareness exercise, is the instrument by which we discover how God has been present to us and how we have responded to that presence through the day.

St. Ignatius believed this practice was so important that, in the event it was impossible to have a formal prayer period, he insisted that the examen would sustain one's vital link with God.

The examen of consciousness is not to be confused with an examination of conscience in which penitents are concerned with their failures. It is, rather, an exploration of how God is present within the events, circumstances, feelings of our daily life.

What the review is to the prayer period, the examen is to our daily life. The daily discipline of an authentic practice of the examen effects the integrating balance that is essential for growth in relationship to God, to self, and to others.

The method reflects the "dynamic movement of personal love: what we always want to say to a person whom we truly love in the order in which we want to say it...Thank you...Help me...I love you...I'm sorry...Be with me" (Cowan and Futrell 1993, 34–35).

Method: The following prayer is a suggested approach to examen. One can incorporate the written responses into one's prayer journal.

- God, my Creator, I am totally dependent on you. Everything is a gift from you.
All is gift. I give you thanks and praise for the gifts of this day...
- Lord, I believe you work through and in time to reveal me to myself. Please give me an increased awareness of how you are guiding and shaping my life, as well as a more sensitive awareness of the obstacles I put in your way.
- You have been present in my life today. Be near, now, as I reflect on these things: your presence in the *events* of today... Your presence in the *feelings* I experienced today your *call* to me....
my response to you...

- God, I ask your loving forgiveness and healing. The particular event of this day for which I most need forgiveness or healing is…
- Filled with hope and a firm belief in your love and power, I entrust myself to your care and strongly affirm…(Claim the gift that you most desire, most need; believe that God desires to give you that gift.)

2. Spiritual Direction, See Appendix C

3. Faith sharing

"For where two or three meet in my name, I am there among them" (Matt. 18:20).

In the creation of community, members must communicate intimately with each other about the core issues of their lives. For the Christian, this is faith sharing and is an extension of daily, solitary prayer.

A faith sharing group is not a discussion group, not a sensitivity session, or a social gathering. Members do not come together to share and receive intellectual or theological insights. Nor is the purpose of faith sharing the accomplishment of some predetermined task.

The purpose of faith sharing is to listen and to be open to God, who continues to be revealed in the church community represented in the small group that comes together in God's name. The fruit of faith sharing is the building up of the Church, the Body of Christ (Eph. 4:12).

The approach to faith sharing is one of reading and reflecting together on the word of God. Faith sharing calls us to share with each other, out of our deepest center, what it means to be a follower of Christ in our world today. To authentically enter into faith sharing is to come to know and love each other in Christ, whose Spirit is the bonding force of community.

An image that faith-sharing groups may find helpful is that of a pool into which pebbles are dropped. The group members gather in a circle and imagine themselves around a pool. Like a pebble being gently dropped into the water, each one offers a reflection—his or her "word" from God. In the shared silence, each offering is received. As the water ripples in concentric circles toward the outer reaches of the pool, so too, this word enlarges and embraces, in love, each member of the circle.

Method: a group of seven to ten members gathers at a prearranged time and place.

- The leader calls the group to prayer and invites members to some moments of silent centering, during which they pray for the presence of the Holy Spirit.
- The leader gathers their silent prayer in an opening prayer, spontaneous or prepared.
- One of the members reads a previously chosen scripture passage on which participants have spent some time in solitary prayer.
- A period of silence follows each reading of the scripture passage.

- The leader invites each one to share a word or phrase from the reading.
- Another member rereads the passage; this is followed by a time of silence.
- The leader invites those who wish to share how this passage personally addresses them, for example, by challenging, comforting, inviting.
- Again, the passage is read.
- Members are invited to offer their spontaneous prayer to the Lord.
- The leader ends the time of faith sharing with a prayer, a blessing, an Our Father, or a hymn.
- Before the group disbands, the passage for the following session is announced.

4. The Role of Imagination in Prayer

Imagination is our power of memory and recall that enables us to enter into the experience of the past and to create the future. Through images we are able to touch the center of who we are and bring to the surface and give life and expression to the innermost levels of our being.

The use of images is important to our psycho-spiritual development. Images simultaneously reveal multiple levels of meaning and are therefore symbolic of our deeper reality.

Through the structured use of active imagination, we release the hidden energy and potential for wholeness that is already present within us.

When we use active imagination in the context of prayer, and with an attitude of faith, we open ourselves to the power and mystery of God's transforming presence within us.

Because the scriptures are, for the most part, a collection of stories and rich in sensual imagery, the use of active imagination in praying the scriptures is particularly enriching. Through the use of imagination, we go beyond the truth of history to discover the truth of the mystery of God's creative word in our life.

5. Coping with Distractions

Do not become overly concerned or discouraged by distractions during prayer. Simply put them aside and return to your prayer material. When a distraction persists, it may be a call to attend prayerfully to the object of the distraction. For example, a conflict may well continue to surface until it has been resolved.

6. Colloquy: Closing Conversational Prayer

St. Ignatius was sensitive to the depth of feeling aroused by the contemplation of the suffering Jesus. Although a suggestion for this intimate conversational prayer at the end of each prayer period has been provided, the one who prays is encouraged to let his or her heart speak in an intimate outpouring of feeling, of love and compassion. One is strongly urged to be *with* Jesus in his resurrection. One may need to pray for the desire to *want* to experience resurrection with Christ. The important thing to remember is that simple presence is primary. Just to be silent in the presence of Christ, resurrected, is profound prayer.

7. Rule of Life

"...your love is before my eyes, and I live my life in loyalty to you." (Ps. 26:3)

People who are serious about their relationship with God, serious about living their lives authentically in tune with the spirit have long recognized the benefit of having a plan of life, sometimes called "a rule of life."

In religious life, this plan has traditionally been called the "Holy Rule." It is a set of principles, guidelines, and practices to which a person commits himself/herself to support a relationship with God, and the charism of the community and its mission.

A plan is not less important for anyone who yearns for an intimate relationship with God, and who is filled with a desire to respond in gratitude for the gifts God has bestowed on them.

A plan can be detailed or very simple. It may include:

A daily schedule with specific times for prayer and other exercises, such as spiritual reading, an examen, the rosary, intercessory prayer as well as a commitment to a compassionate care of self with a balance of and rhythm of work, rest, and leisure.

A weekly or monthly schedule of attendance at Mass, the sacrament of reconciliation, spiritual direction, the prayerful celebration of the liturgical feasts and seasons. It would include an annual retreat.

A rule of life includes the goals one has, that is, how one is being called to grow in specific areas of one's life. The goals should be stated in such a way that they are:

"Specific: Are my spiritual goals precise, detailed and explicit?

Measurable: Have I stated my spiritual goals clearly enough that I can take daily steps toward achieving them?

Realistic: Are my spiritual goals high but within reach of someone with my responsibilities as a mother/father, wife/husband/religious/priest/single/ lay person, and so forth?" (Burke 2012, p. 118)

Having a rule of life offers the additional benefit of a guideline for discernment, for reflecting periodically on one's faithfulness or lack thereof, and the need to revise one's direction. Regular periodic, times of reflection on one's goals fosters obedience to God's call within one's committed state of life. The discernment can also serve as a springboard for sharing with one's spiritual director.

Point 1

Love in Deed Not Only in Word

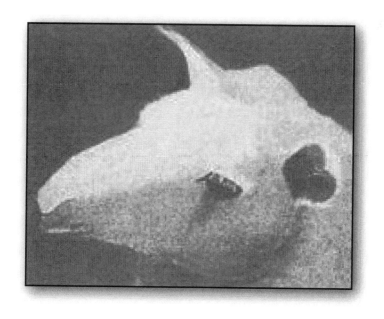

before beginning, two observations should be noted:

+ Love ought to show itself in deeds over and above words;

+ Love consists in a mutual sharing of goods.

For example, a lover gives and shares with the beloved something of his personal gifts or some possession which he has or is able to give; so, too, the beloved shares with the lover. In this way, one who has knowledge shares it with one who does not, and this is true for honors, riches, and so on. In love, one always wants to give to the other.

Spiritual Exercises, # 230-231

FROM LOVE, IN LOVE, TO LOVE

Psalm 63:1–8

God, you are my God, I am seeking you, my soul is thirsting for you. My flesh is longing for you, a land parched, weary and water less; I long to gaze on you in the sanctuary, and to see your power and glory.

Your love is better than life itself, my lips will recite your praise; all my life I will bless you, in your name lift up my hands; my soul will feast most richly, on my lips a song of joy and, in my mouth, praise.

On my bed I think of you, I meditate on you all night long, for you have always helped me, I sing for joy in the shadow of your wings; my soul clings close to you, your right hand supports me.

Commentary:

"They asked the Lover where he was from. " From love." "What are you made of?" "Love." "Who Conceived you?" "Love." "Where were you born?" "In love." "Who raised you?" "Love." "What do you live on?" "Love." "What is your name?" "Love" "Where do you come from?" "Love." "Where are you going?" "To love." "Where are you?" "In love." "Do you have anything besides love?" He replied: "Yes, my sins and offenses against my Beloved." "Does your Beloved pardon you?" The Lover said there was mercy and justice in his Beloved. And so he found shelter between fear and hope." (Ramon Llull, 10, Ilia Delio, OSF, *Clare of Assisi: A Heart Full of Love*)

In the thirteenth century, the Spanish mystic Ramon Llull penned these words, embracing the heart of spirituality, underscoring the centrality of God's love.

Two hundred years later, St. Ignatius framed his Spiritual Exercises in this same love. As a preliminary to the Exercises, Ignatius invites the retreatant to ponder a statement on the purpose of each person "to praise, reverence and serve God," that is to love God. That God's all-embracing love is the principal and foundation of all of life is captured in a prayer that paraphrases Ignatius's own words, "Lord, my God, when your love spilled over into creation, you thought of me. I am from love, of love, for love" (Bergan and Schwan 1985,2004, 8).

God is Love loving, Giver giving. It is from this fountain fullness of love that all creation has been brought forth, and it is within this ongoing extravagance that all of creation is sustained.

The psalmist gives word to the poignant hunger and thirst that is the deep poverty of the human condition. It is this poverty that leads to a recognition of our total dependence on God. The gift of this awareness reminds us constantly that apart from God, we are nothing. It tells us that we are not here because we chose to be, that it is not even necessary that we exist, and that every breath we breathe is dependent on God. It is only through the gracious love of God that we have life and have been placed within this created world. In the acknowledgement of our poverty, of our dependence on God, our hearts are filled with gratitude. Everything has been and continues to be gift, and God is the Giver. "Your love is better than life itself."

We do "long to gaze," "to see," and so to be transformed into the love that is poured into our hearts. And so, at the end of the Exercises, in the Exercise called the "Contemplation to Attain Divine Love," Ignatius makes this same love the principal and foundation of a life that will be lived, day in and day out, in discipleship, in laboring with and for Christ.

In the words of Pope Francis, "True love is always contemplative, and permits us to serve the other, not out of necessity or vanity, but rather because he or she is beautiful above and beyond mere appearances" (Pope Francis, 101).

In the beautiful prose of Robert Sardello's book, *Silence: The Mystery of Wholeness*, we are called to pray within the deep silence of our hearts. Sardello assures us that, "The comfort that appears when we pray within Silence is a powerful force. We feel held by a completely loving and understanding presence, which has the power of removing all fear and anguish. Such praying does not take away what we are given to bear, but the way we bear it radically changes. Instead of a burden of heaviness, the difficulty has been lifted into the light. The task we are now given is to remember this light....We may still feel fear, but it no longer dominates and has no power over us. In fact, we feel joy....This joy is not an emotion but the very nature of the comforting community of prayer. No matter how difficult things are, this sense of the power of comfort persists. (Sardello 2008, 119)

It is in contemplative receptivity that we discover the transformative empowerment and joy of the gift of Divine love.

From Love, In Love, To Love

Suggested approach to prayer: I Am Seeking You

+ Daily prayer plan (Orientations p.xxxi)

I quiet myself and relax in the presence of God. I declare my dependency on God.

+ Grace: I beg for the gift of an intimate knowledge of the sharing of good that God does in God's love for me. Filled with gratitude, I desire to love God and my neighbor "not only in word or in the experience of some tender moment of love but also…in deed and in truth…" (Medaille 1979).

Method: Meditative Reading (Orientations p.xxxiiii)

— Reverently pray and repray Psalm 63:1-8
— Allow the words to wash over you. Be attentive to any memories or feelings that the words illicit.
— Consider memorizing the psalm and incorporate it into your evening prayer.

+ As the end of prayer draws to a conclusion, spend twenty minutes in quiet contemplative prayer.

+ Close your prayer time with an Our Father.

+ Review of prayer: Record in your journal the thoughts and feelings that have surfaced during your prayer.

From Love, In Love, To Love

Complimentary Prayer: Prayer of Praise

+ In this prayer period, use the introductory and closing framework of the previous prayer.

+ Prayerfully read and reread the following prayer, based on the Principle and Foundation of the Spiritual Exercises:

*Lord my God, when your love spilled over into creation
You thought of me. I am*

    From love   of love   for love

.

*Let my heart, O God, always
   recognize,
   cherish,
   and enjoy your goodness in all of creation.*

*Direct all that is me toward your praise.
Teach me reverence for every person, all things. Energize me in your service.*

*Lord God, may nothing ever distract me from your love…
   neither health nor sickness
   wealth nor poverty
   honor nor dishonor
   long life nor short life.*

May I never seek nor choose to be other
  than You intend or wish.   Amen.

+ In turn, pray this prayer as a prayer of praise,
    as a prayer of thanksgiving,
    as a prayer of petition.

+ If moved to do so, gently and softly sing the prayer, making up your own melody.

The Scarlet Thread

Luke 6:36

Be compassionate as God is compassionate.

Commentary:

At the heart of the Gospel is the call to compassion. It is ever new, yet rooted in the most ancient of Jewish traditions. It is woven through the long and intricate history, through the unfolding riches of God's word like a scarlet thread.

> Jesus did not simply reproduce and repeat the Old Testament. He certainly did not insert completely new content into it. Instead, from the immense material in his Bible, from this experience of the centuries, from this heaped-up mass of wisdom and history he discerned and drew out the scarlet thread of God's will—with a sensitivity and ability to distinguish that we can only marvel at. (Lohfink 2012, 187)

When Jesus appeared on the scene of history, Judean religious practice was at a low point of legalism. Religious leaders multiplied laws that governed and oppressed the people who often as not did not know what the laws entailed. Those who did not know and practice the detailed practices were considered sinners.

Jesus, with his parents, was a part of the remnant, promised in Zephaniah 3:12, "a humble and lowly people...who seek refuge in the name of Yahweh…" They lived, faithful to the Law, but primarily faithful to its deeper meaning, the spirit of the Law.

The scarlet thread that twines through the scriptures that Jesus heard, read, memorized, and made his own, is the revelation of a God, who through the history of his people, cared for and, even in the face of the gross infidelity of the people, continually drew near to them in forgiveness. It became apparent to Israel that it was God's faithful and loving compassion that called them in the call to Abraham—that drew them out of the oppression of Egypt and guided them through the desert, into the promised land, and brought them home again from exile. God's love was always greater than their own infidelity.

The words Jesus found repeatedly in the psalms and in stories that originally and most authentically shaped the religious experience of the people were *hesido loolam*… a forever, faithful love, a love that is better translated as loving, tender kindness.

A wonderful example is found in Psalm 136, a litany of the great deeds of God in the history of his people. Each remembrance is celebrated with the refrain…*for his great love is without end*… In all the events of life, even when they were most unfaithful, the Jewish people recognized and claimed the enduring and faithful love of their God. They experienced it as compassion.

The Hebrew word for compassion, in its singular form, means "womb." "To say that God is compassionate is to say that God is 'like a womb,' 'is womblike'…….In its sense of 'like a womb,' *compassion* has nuances of giving life, nourishing, caring, perhaps embracing, and encompassing. For Jesus, this is what God is like" (Borg 1994, 48).

This is the God Jesus knew and loved. Having reappropriated this deep and authentic understanding of God, his own life became a witness to it, one might say a sacrament of it. This is the good news he shared with his countrymen and women, through his words and through his deeds.

Be compassionate as God is compassionate. Who God is and how we are to live came together in the life of Jesus as it must in our own lives.

The Scarlet Thread

Suggested approach to prayer: Steadfast and Faithful Is God's Love

+ Daily prayer plan (Orientations p.xxxi)

I quiet myself and relax in the presence of God. I declare my dependency on God.

+ Grace: Ask for the grace of a deepening awareness of the compassion of God as the root and foundation of your life.

In Psalm 117, we find the phrase, "Faithful is God's Love." It can be expanded to read "Steadfast and faithful, God's tender, loving tender kindness." Pray these words as a mantra, letting the words wash over you, and enter into your deepest awareness.

Close by praying and perhaps memorizing Psalm 117:

Praise God, all you nations.
Praise God, all you peoples.
Faithful and steadfast God's tender, loving kindness.
Praise God.

+ As the time of your prayer draws to a conclusion, spend twenty minutes in quiet contemplative prayer.

+ Close your prayer with an Our Father.

+ Review of Prayer: Record in your journal the thoughts and feelings that have surfaced during your prayer.

From the Beginning

John 1:1, 14

> In the beginning was the Word;
> the Word was with God
> and the Word was God…
>
> The Word was made flesh,
> he lived among us,
> and we saw his glory,
> the glory that is his as the only Son of the Father,
> full of grace and truth.

Commentary:

"When the Word becomes flesh, God bends over in love to lift up not only human nature but creation itself…" (Delio 2005, 5)

From the beginning, God speaks his Word of love. With the opening of his Gospel, John plunges us and all of creation into the very center, the inner dynamic of God's love, his Word made flesh in the person and spirit of Jesus Christ. From the very beginning, all of creation, the entire universe was, and is now, orientated toward Christ.

Teilhard de Chardin, twentieth-century prophetic mystic and paleontologist, sees Christ as the Alpha and Omega, the beginning and the fulfillment of all Creation, "a Christ centered universe as an evolutionary universe moving towards the fullness of Christ" (Delio 2005, 3).

The Word becoming flesh, the Incarnation, is the self-diffusive, bubbling over of God's love like a spectacular fountain spilling over in creative love. All of creation is the expression of this great spilling over of God's goodness and love.

For the Hebrew people, "word" was not only a spoken or written word, as we have a tendency to think of it. The word extended to actions—as when one reaches out to shake a hand in greeting—and things, like a gift that "speaks" to us. So God communicates to his faithful through events and all of creation as well as the revelatory word spoken by prophets and priests. We have only to listen. All of creation and all of history are the expression of this great spilling over of God's goodness and love.

Christ, the Word of God, the son of God, was God's intention from the beginning. Christ is the expression of God's creative love for all of us. God did not send Jesus, primarily, as a consequence of sin, but, rather, the Word was made flesh out of God's great and loving desire to be one with creation. Christ is the unimaginable gift of the Father to all of creation. "Once we restore the idea that the Incarnation means that God truly loves creation then we restore the sacred dimension to nature...the material and spiritual co-exist...'Nature offers us windows' into the endless creativity, fruitfulness and joy of God" (Rohr, source unknown).

Out of great tenderness, God sent Christ to lift us up. In Christ, God bends low to meet us where we are, in the circumstances and events of our lives. God's love embraces our every frailty, confusion, and weakness. God is in our joy as well as in our suffering.

God bends low in love!

From the Beginning

Suggested approach to prayer: The Loving Plan of God

+ Daily prayer plan (Orientations xxxi)

I quiet myself and relax in the presence of God. I declare my dependency on God.

Grace: I beg for the gift of an intimate knowledge of the sharing of goods that God does in his love for me. Filled with gratitude, I desire to love God and my neighbor "not only in word or in the experience of some tender moment of love but also…in deed and in truth…"

Method: Meditation (Orientations p.xxxiv)

(Adapted from *Spiritual Exercises*, paras. 101–109)

I see and consider the three persons of the Trinity—God our Creator, God the Son, and God the Holy Spirit—as they lovingly look upon our world.

I try to enter into the vision of our universe as God sees it.

I see the earth with all its plants and animals. I see the earth in all its grandeur and I see as well the scars that have been inflicted upon it by the abuse of human thoughtlessness and exploitation.

I see all the men, women, and children who comprise our global
  community. I see people in all stages of their lives. Some are
  being born, some being married, some giving birth as well as
  those who are elderly and dying. I see those who are struggling
  with the devastation of poverty, war, and injustice. I see them all:
  those filled with tears, those overjoyed with happiness.

I see God's great love and compassion for all.

I see the time has come; God has a plan. The plan is about to be
fulfilled.

"God has let us know the mystery of his purpose, the hidden plan
  God so kindly made in Christ from the beginning to act upon
  when the times have run their course to the end: that God
  would bring everything together under Christ as head, everything in the heavens and everything on earth." (Eph. 1:9–10)

I stay with the vision of God.

I see the angel Gabriel approach Mary. I see her surprise. I hear
  her questions. I see her reassured by Gabriel.

With God, I wait for her response.

In gratitude, I let my heart respond to God.

+ As the time of my prayer draws to a conclusion, I spend twenty
  minutes in quiet contemplative prayer.

+ I close my prayer time with an Our Father.

+ Review of Prayer: I record in my journal the thoughts and feelings that have surfaced during my prayer.

From the Beginning

Complimentary prayer: Incarnation

+ Method: Poetry as Prayer (Orientations p.xxxix)

In this prayer period, use the introductory and closing framework of the previous prayer.

+ Prayerfully read and reread the following poem.

Incarnation

God held in his hand
A small globe. Look, he said.
The son looked. Far off,
As though through water, he saw
A scorched land of fierce
Colour. The light burned
There; crusted buildings
Cast their shadows; a bright
Serpent, a river,
Uncoiled itself, radiant with slime.

On a bare Hill
a bare tree saddened the sky.
Many people Held out their thin arms To it,
as though waiting For a vanished April
To return to its crossed
Boughs. The son watched
Them. Let me go there, he said.

(R. S. Thomas, a Welsh Anglican
priest of the twentieth century)

+ Enter into the poem, imaging each line, entering each scene.

+ See God holding the earth like a small globe in his hand.

+ Listen as God says, "Look." What does the Son see? What do you see?

+ The Son says that he will "go there." What is your call?

And the Word was made flesh.

The Visitation

Luke 2:39–45

> Mary set out at that time and went as quickly as she could to a town in a hill country of Judah. She went into Zechariah's house and greeted Elizabeth. Now as soon as Elizabeth heard Mary's greeting, the child leapt in her womb and Elizabeth was filled with the Holy Spirit. She gave a loud cry and said, "Of all women, you are the most blessed, and blessed is the fruit of your womb. Why should I be honored with a visit from the mother of my Lord?" For the moment your greeting reached my ears, the child in my womb leapt for joy. Yes, blessed is she who believed that the promise made her by the Lord would be fulfilled.

Commentary:

"It is not in soul-searching or constant introspection that we encounter the Lord…" said Pope Francis in his homily at the Chrism Mass during Holy Week. "Grace," he said, "comes alive and flourishes to the extent that we, in faith, go out and give ourselves and the Gospel to others."

Mary anticipated the words of the newly elected leader of the Church. No sooner than Mary hears that her cousin, Elizabeth, is pregnant than she, herself, in the fresh awareness of her own incredible pregnancy, sets out "as quickly as she could" to make the long journey to Hebron in the mystery of an encounter that we know as the Visitation.

In the meeting and embrace of Mary and Elizabeth, it is as if we can hear God laughing with delight. Two women one old, beyond the time of bearing children, the other, young, unwed and pregnant.

They were two ordinary women, who were not very significant in first-century Israel. Religion had lost its vibrancy and the hope held out by the prophets. Legalism had overtaken religious practices that had become heavy and oppressive as religious leaders strove to impose authority and control. People were filled with fear of the terrorism that often erupted into bloodshed.

But here are two women, Mary and Elizabeth, and two men, Joseph and Zachary, and two unborn children. The two families are a part of the small community of the anawim, that remnant of the faithful, who in the midst of the chaos of the times continued to believe, to trust, not in horses or chariots or riches or power, but in the promise of God (Zeph. 3:11–13).

The scene is like an icon for us to contemplate: two women meeting, greeting, embracing each other. Elizabeth after years of disappointment and discouragement, beyond the time of conceiving and giving birth, is thrilled as she prepares for the birth of her son. Mary, no doubt pondering the mystery that is unfolding within her, reaches out to bring support and care to her older pregnant cousin.

The child within Elizabeth leaps with recognition of the Presence within Mary. Not yet fully formed, Jesus is already the source of life. And these two women will give life to the sacred stories that shape their lives in their service to each other.

Wise Elizabeth recognizes, as holy people always do, that in Mary God is profoundly at work, shaping the future.

In describing the visitation, St. Luke draws on the imagery of the Ark of the Covenant. In Exodus, Moses was instructed to make an ark of acacia wood, to line it with gold, and to place within in the ten commandments, that is, the covenant between God and Israel, and a vessel of manna. Here God would be present. The Ark was carried by the people in their journeying in the desert, until it would be placed in the Temple, in the Holy of Holies. When David wanted to establish Jerusalem as the capital and center of his nation, he went to the house of Obed-Edom where the Ark had remained for three months. Then, David, led the procession, taking the Ark to the future sight of the Temple in Jerusalem.

Mary is the new Ark of the Covenant. She carried within her the Lord of the Covenant, as she traveled south to Hebron, where she remained for three month.

In the meeting of these two holy women, grace came alive and "flourished."

The Visitation

Suggested approach to prayer: Being with Mary

+ Daily prayer plan (Orientations p. xxxi)

I quiet myself and relax in the presence of God. I declare my dependency on God.

Grace: I beg for the gift of an intimate knowledge of the sharing of goods that God does in his love for me. Filled with gratitude, I desire to love God and my neighbor "not only in word or in the experience of some tender moment of love but also...in deed and in truth..."

Method: Ignatian Contemplation   (Orientations p.xxxiv)

+ Prayerfully reread the passage and the commentary.

+ Let the story unfold in your imagination. See yourself in the scene, possibly as a companion to Mary as she prepares for and sets out on the journey to Hebron.

See yourself and Mary as part of a caravan.

See Mary as she says good-bye to her parents, and to Joseph.

What is the spring weather like?

What is the country, and the villages, like, through which you pass?

What is the exchange between you and Mary, and with the other travelers?

See Mary as she approaches the home of Elizabeth and Zachary, and the greeting between the two women.

Ponder the mystery and the beauty and the love of their sharing.

Let yourself imagine what those three months were like—the conversations between the two women, each sharing her fears, her hopes, her joys.

+ As the time of my prayer draws to a conclusion, I spend twenty minutes in quiet contemplative prayer

+ I close my prayer time with an Our Father.

+ Review of Prayer: I record in my journal the thoughts and feelings that have surfaced during my prayer.

The Visitation

Complimentary prayer: Mary Prayed

+ In this prayer period, use the introductory and closing framework of the previous prayer.

As Elizabeth greeted her younger cousin, Mary, in the spirit of her foremother Hanna (1 Sam. 2:1–10), breaks out into a prayer and song of praise.

+ Prayerfully, read and pray each line, with an awareness of the mystery of the Word becoming flesh not only in the flesh of Mary, but in all of creation:

My soul proclaims the greatness of the Lord and
my spirit exults in God my savior:
because he has looked upon his lowly handmaid.
Yes, from this day forward all generations will call me
blessed,
for the almighty has done great things for me.
Holy is his name,
and his mercy reaches from age to age for those
who fear him.
He has shown the power of his arm, he has route the
proud of
heart. He has pulled down princes from their thrones and
exalted
the lowly. He has come to the help of Israel his servant,
and mindful of his mercy

according to the promise he made to our ancestors. Of his mercy to Abraham [and Sarah] and to his descendents forever.

+ What is the Word from this reading that is an invitation to you to translate it into action?

The Lavish Gift

1 John 3:1

> Think of the love the Father has lavished on us, by letting us be called God's children; and that is what we are.

Commentary:

In the mystery of infinite mercy and tenderness, God continually brings forth and sustains us as beloved children.

> When Israel was a child I loved him...
> I myself taught Ephraim to walk, I took him in my arms...
> I was like someone who lifts an infant close against his cheek; stooping down to him I gave him his food. (Hosea 11:1, 3, 4)

God, in all the fullness of love, shares God's very being with us. This is what it means to be God's children. Those to whom we give birth in our human experience share our DNA, the very core reality of our being.

So, too, and infinitely more, God shares God's own essential life with us.

> Our existence is...in God. The relationship between God and [us], therefore, instead of being of pure transcendence (which does not admit any relation) is one of immanence.

God is the transcendent mystery immanent in us. (Panikar 2004, 22–23)

God is not something or someone "out there," beyond our experience, beyond our "knowing." God is here and now! God's loving presence penetrates us. God is in us and we are in God. We are truly created "in the image and likeness of God" (Gen. 1:27). Yet, God remains God and we are who we are, a finite expression of the infinite.

The discovery of ourselves as God's children changes everything. "We see ourselves as being a created act of God, simply unique and absolutely precious" (Bruteau 2002, 68). This reassurance is given to us in Isaiah, "…you are precious in my sight, honored and I love you…" (Isa. 43:4).

As a child of God, we embrace an entire new identity. We no longer live out of the old story, the old identity, for example, that we are intrinsically flawed, or that we are what we possess, or that we are what we do, or that we are how the world evaluates us. To see oneself as a beloved child of God, as one whom God "lifts [as] an infant close against his cheek," is a complete reorientation. It is to claim and enter into a new way of being.

With the psalmist, we declare:

I am filled with love, for the Lord hears me:
the Lord bends to my voice whenever I call. (Ps. 116:1–2)

The Lavish Gift

Suggested approach to prayer: Into the New Story

+ Daily prayer plan (Orientations p.xxxi)

I quiet myself and relax in the presence of God. I declare my dependency on God.

+ Grace: I beg for the gift of an intimate knowledge of the sharing of goods that God does in God's love for me. Filled with gratitude, I desire to love God and my neighbor "not only in word or in the experience of some tender moment of love but also…in deed and in truth…"

Method: Lectio Divina   (Orientations p.xxxvi)

Prayerfully reread the scripture:

> Think of the love the Father has lavished on us, by letting us be called God's children; and that is what we are. (1 John 3:1)

+ Repeatedly read aloud the passage, each time emphasizing a different word, for example,

> *Think* of the love of the Father…

> Think of the *love* of the Father…

+ Consider:

    What resonates within you?
    What experiences come to your mind and heart?

+ What is your prayerful response? Thanksgiving? Praise? Petition?

+ Simply rest in any interior movement you experience.

Given a deeper awareness of yourself as a child of God, intimately loved and held, what difference will it make? Can you claim and trust this gift and its altering and transforming power in your life? Can you live out of this news story?

In gratitude, let your heart respond.

+ As the time of prayer draws to a conclusion, spend twenty minutes in quiet contemplative prayer.

+ Close your prayer time with an Our Father.

+ Review of Prayer: Record in your journal the thoughts and feelings that have surfaced during your prayer.

Loved and Loving

1 John 3:18

> My children, our love is not to be just words or mere talk, but something real and active; only by *this* can we be certain that we are children of the truth.

Commentary:

"Words, words, words. I'm so tired of words. Don't tell me you love me. Show me"
(*My Fair Lady*, lyrics by Alan Jay Lerner).

We, too, are tired of words without substance, words that are empty of deeds of love.

In spite of all the efforts being made throughout the world to bring renewal and peace, *it* often seems that we have lost love as the center of our culture. When the mind is divorced from the heart, devastation follows; society collapses. We see and personally experience this collapse all around us. We feel its sting within our families, and we are filled with sadness and disappointment in the realization of the dysfunction of our societal structures upon which we have depended. Many of our institutions are no longer supportive or life giving. Collapse is everywhere. It is a global phenomenon.

As children of a loving God, what is our response? We are a people whose God is a God of love revealed in Jesus Christ, active and present. As children of *this* loving, present, and active God, what do we have to bring to the chaos that marks our times? We see in the Epistle of John our love is not to be just words or talk but something real and active.

John invites us to fail in love. True love is always real and active. Once we fall in love and we genuinely love another we are transformed. Nothing is ever the same! Those who love each other, live in each other and for each other. They enjoy, they laugh, they suffer, and they cry together. They are, in a sense, of one spirit, penetrated with the gift of each other. All their words and deeds flow from this love for each other. Their desire is for a limitless self-giving.

Love changes us. It empowers our truest selves. Hopefully, we can all remember a time or event when we were affirmed and transformed in love. An elderly woman recalls when on her confirmation day her father introduced her as "my beautiful daughter." Those simple words of a loving father to his young daughter released her from the awkwardness of adolescence into the true beauty of her young womanhood. In a brief moment, she was given "a new story." Freed and empowered to move from a limiting self-consciousness into confidence, from that day forward she lived her life from the center of beauty affirmed by her father. From that center, she was empowered to affirm others in their beauty. Until we know that we are loved we are frozen in a paralysis of inaction. It is essential that we discover ourselves as loved.

Whatever our experiences of human love, precious as they are, they are a microcosm of the magnanimity of God's love and its great power of transforming us. In discovering ourselves as God's children, we have been taken over and penetrated by a powerful reality that changes us.

We are living in what is called a paradigm shift, a time of great change, when we witness the decline of our global culture and an environmental crisis. Though we do not yet see what newness is emerging, we are filled with a great desire to make our own contribution to the evolution of a new paradigm, a new way of understanding. Finally, in the midst of the chaos, we are ultimately dependent upon the guidance of the Spirit and can rest in the assurance of the promise of the Spirit's creating presence. It is our task to be quiet enough to hear God's voice within and courageous enough to act.

> Glory be to God whose power, working in us, can do infinitely more than we can ask or imagine; glory be to Him from generation to generation in the Church and in Christ Jesus, forever and ever. Amen. (Eph. 3:20–21)

Loved and Loving

Suggested approach to prayer: Love's Mirror

+ Daily prayer plan (Orientations p.xxxi)

I quiet myself and relax in the presence of God. I declare my dependency on God.

Grace: I beg for the gift of an intimate knowledge of the sharing of goods that God does in God's love for me. Filled with gratitude, I desire to love God and my neighbor "not only in word or in the experience of some tender moment of love by also…in deed and in truth…"

Method: Meditation (Orientations p. xxxiv)

Nothing is more practical than finding God,
than falling in love in a quite absolute final way.

What you are in love with, what seizes your imagination, will affect everything.

It will decide what will get you out of bed in the morning, how you spend your week-end, what you read, who you know, what breaks your heart and what amazes with joy and gratitude.

Fall in love, stay in love, and it will decide everything.

(Pedro Arrupe, SJ)

Recall and reflect on a personal experience of falling in love. How did it alter your life? How does your experience of love mirror God's love for you and your loving of God?

In gratitude, I thank God for how love has touched my life and changed me.

+ As the time of my prayer draws to a conclusion, spend twenty minutes in quiet contemplative prayer.

+ Close your prayer with an Our Father.

+ Review of Prayer: Record in your journal the thoughts and feelings that have surfaced during your prayer.

God's People

Ezekiel 37:26–27

> I shall make a covenant of peace with them…I shall settle my sanctuary among them forever…I will be their God, and they shall be my people.

Commentary:

God's love is relational.

God's love is uniquely revealed in community.

From the beginning, God entered into relationship with the Hebrew people as a community. "They shall be my people and I will be their God" (Jer. 24:7). God's covenant, frequently renewed at critical points in their history, gave Israel a sense of identity, purpose, and cohesiveness. When the people found themselves at odds with each other, it was the covenant with God that served to bring them back together again. The Israelites had a deep awareness that it was God who took the initiative in making of them a people of election, God's people.

In times of conflict, the prophets called on the remembrance of the covenant as a way of reconciling and reuniting the dissonant factions. Ezekiel was the prophet who accompanied his people into exile and back again. One of the rich symbolic stories illustrating God's desire for unity among the people is the story of how Ezekiel took two sticks, one representing the southern kingdom of Judah and the other representing the remaining members of the northern kingdom. Ezekiel was instructed to go before the people, not simply to talk about unity, but by holding the two sticks together to concretely illustrate that "the Lord Yahweh says...I will make them into one nation in my own land... they will no longer form two nations.......I shall make a covenant of peace with them, an eternal covenant with them...I will be their God, and they shall be my people.

...God unites, by the positive energy of loving, 'shepherding,' and revealing the Divine Presence in one's midst and between them...God's continual job description, it seems is mimed in the two bound sticks of Ezekiel. God is always and forever making one out of two." (Rohr 2011, 119–20)

God never forgot God's people. God is master over human history. Over and again as they faced collapse, against all odds, God intervened. God raised up men like Ezekiel and women prophets who were instruments in reconciling, reuniting, renewing, and redirecting God's people.

Always God brought the people home making of them God's dwelling place. "I shall settle my sanctuary among them forever" (Ezek. 37:27).

As the people returned from exile, they experienced a new moment in their story. God was saying to them through the prophet, "I will bring you home to your own land. I shall pour clean water over you and you will be cleansed; I shall cleanse you of all your defilement and all your idols. I shall give you a new heart, and put a new spirit in you; I shall remove the heart of stone from your bodies and give you a heart of flesh instead…You shall be my people and I will be your God" (Ezek. 36:24–26, 28).

How do we, people of the twenty-first century, people who claim to believe in a faithful loving God, dare to live without hope? As New Testament people, with the spirit of Jesus Christ dwelling within us, can we embrace trust? Grounded in the consciousness of our covenant in and through Christ, can we allow ourselves to be empowered as instruments of hope in our time?

We *can* live out of the new story of what it means to be God's people.

God's People

Suggested approach to prayer: Called Home

+ Daily prayer plan (Orientations p.xxxi)

I quiet myself and relax in the presence of God. I declare my dependency on God.

+ Grace: I beg for the gift of an intimate knowledge of the sharing of goods that God does in God's love for me. Filled with gratitude, I desire to love God and my neighbor "not only in word or in the experience of some tender moment of love but also...in deed and in truth..."

Method: Meditation (Orientations p.xxxiv)

The people in Ezekiel's time experienced both exile and homecoming. They were separated from their country and their God. Paradoxically, it was in exile that they came to a new awareness of God's saving presence in their lives.

+ Where in the circumstances and events of your life have you experienced "exile," for example, times of being overwhelmed with fear, grief, or self-doubt?

+ Have there been times when you have experienced being separated from God and from your true self by substance addiction or process addictions, such as overwork, over activity, and overconsumption?

+ When has God, seemingly against all odds, come to your rescue? Think of the many times throughout your history that God has intervened and surprised you with the gift of healing and hope and restored you to inner peace. Savor the memory of these times.

+ Claim as your own the covenanting words of God, "You are my people; I am your God."

+ As the time of my prayer draws to a conclusion, I spend twenty minutes in quiet contemplative prayer.

+ Close your prayer with an Our Father.

+ Review of prayer: Record in your journal the thoughts and feelings that have surfaced during your prayer.

God's People

Complimentary prayer: Against All Odds

+For this prayer period, use the introductory and closing framework of the previous prayer..

+ Enter into the celebration of God's unfailing care by introducing each of the unfolding parts of the prayer of Zachary (Luke 1:68 ff.). Pray his words slowly, reflectively, letting the Word shape your reflection.

> Praise the Lord, the God of Israel,
> who shepherds the people and sets them free.
>
> **Against all odds,**
> God raises from David's house a child with power to save.
> Through the holy prophets God promised in ages past
> to save us from enemy hands, from the grip of all who hate
> us.
>
> **Against all odds,**
> The Lord favored our ancestors recalling the sacred covenant,
> the pledge to our ancestor Abraham, to free us from our enemies,
> so we might worship without fear and be holy and just all our days.

Against all odds,
And you, child, will be called Prophet of the Most High,
for you will come to prepare a pathway for the Lord
by teaching the people salvation through forgiveness of
their sins.

Against all odds,
Out of God's deepest mercy a dawn will come from on high,
light for those shadowed by death,
a guide for our feet on the way to peace.

Glory be to the Father, to the Son and to the Holy Spirit
as it was in the beginning, is now and ever shall be
world without end.   Amen.

Conversion and Transformation

Wisdom 7:27b

> In each generation Wisdom passes into holy souls, she makes them friends of God and prophets.

Commentary:

To begin to think of ourselves as "God's people," and individually as God's beloved daughter or son is to enter into a new story of oneself–to enter into the process of conversion, typically a long slow transformation that is accompanied by the painful surrender of previous images of identity that have formed our concept of who we are and our place in the world.

Our understanding of personal conversion can be enriched by studying the great spiritual masters of our tradition. Invariably, we see that their realization and embracing of themselves as a child of God was formed by circumstances and events of their lives that stripped them of their dependency on narcissistic world values of pride, possessions, and power or as Marcus Borg calls it, the three As: attention, affection, and affluence. For most of us, it is in and through diminishment that we begin to grow into maturity and the acceptance, internal integration, and realization of spiritual values. In the surrender of who we think we are we become who we truly are—God's beloved.

This experience is seen clearly in the conversion of St. Paul.

Throughout Judeo-Christian history, God has raised up men and women who would be instruments in his hand, who would not only articulate but also live the Word of God among the people. Always, in the covenant community, there are leaders, who shaped by the Word, that is, the Wisdom of God, announce the plan of God.

Outstanding among the leaders in the early Christian community was the apostle Paul. Until the moment when he was thrown to the ground and met Christ in a blinding light, Paul was a dedicated Jew, a Pharisee. Young, strong, a Jew with Greek family connections and a Roman citizen, Saul was the "renaissance man" of his time. He was a promising leader in the Jewish community, not only learned in the Law, but with a clear mission to clear out the fledgling community of Christians in Damascus. Someone has said that his life with the experiences that had formed him, and the gifts that he had honed was like a mirror.

Then came the blinding light that forced Paul to the ground, and the voice, "Saul, Saul, why are you persecuting me?" "Who are you, Lord?" "I am Jesus of Nazareth and you are persecuting me" (Acts 9:4–5). That word transformed Paul's life.

Suddenly the mirror of his life lay in shattered pieces at his feet. The absolute certainty, the unquestioned clarity, were as broken pieces. He went from being a persecutor of Christians to being a disciple of Jesus and an apostle. Paul's plan gave way to God's plan.

As Paul Tillich has said, Saul-become-Paul never put the pieces together again. It was the love of Christ that held his life together. Every learning, every experience of his life, found its way into his ministry in the Name and Spirit of Christ. What might have seemed as the greatest loss was found again in Christ.

The Word continued to form the apostle Paul through love and suffering, like the two hands of God shaping his life. Paul would know his share of love as the Christian community eventually embraced him, and were even reduced to tears when he left them (Acts 20:36–37). And he himself tells us of the sufferings that formed him as he recounts that he endured imprisonment many times over, whippings, and beating, stoning, shipwreck, and the like (2 Cor. 11:23).

Through it all, the Word was made flesh in him and through him as he traveled the known world preaching the Good News of the Gospel.

God had shaped Paul and transformed him into a servant and witness to the Word.

Not unlike Paul, Ignatius of Loyola experienced a dramatic life-changing conversion.

Ignatius was born into a world "dominated by forceful personalities, staunch family traditions and loyalties, and values and ideals that extended back to the furthest reaches of memory and legend" (Meissner 1992, 3).

Ignatius was born in 1491, a historical time in which the excitement and turmoil of revolution, reformation, and discovery prevailed. Formed as he was by the proud and independent character of his family, the circumstances of the times fueled Ignatius's competitive and overly ambitious nature. As a young man, he threw himself into the life of a single courtier; he gambled, brawled, womanized, and sought every occasion to raise his sword in a duel. His life and identity focused on his physical appearance and strength of conquest. He was Ignatius—the handsome, proud, and invincible warrior!

On May 20, 1517, during the battle of Pamplona, while fighting against a besieging French army of twelve thousand, a cannonball shattered Ignatius's right leg and badly injured the left. Ignatius's wounds were severe, and he endured a long torturous period of recovery. Things would never be as they had been; he would never be the same! It was not only his body that was shattered but even more significant was the shattering of his self-image. Ignatius would no longer be the virile, handsome military hero.

It was during his long recuperation that Ignatius discovered and grew in his own sense of identity. In the painful diminishment of self, in the letting go of all he thought himself to be "he grew in the internal realization of a deeper, fuller, more realistic and more spiritual system of values" (Missner, 400).

The period of recuperation was a time of extraordinary healing for Ignatius. His sister-in-law, Magdalena, a devoted and skilled caregiver, played a crucial role in Ignatius's restoration of health.

The recuperation of Ignatius's went, however, beyond his physical health. Ignatius had endured the emotional trauma of having been deprived of his mother's love when she died shortly after his birth. There was a way in which Magdalena, through her attentive care of him, was instrumental, to a significant degree, in nurturing the healing of that deep pain. Not only did Magdalena's care serve to facilitate Ignatius's physical and emotional health but also it was she who set him on his spiritual path when she offered, for his reading, the books on the life of Christ and the life of the saints. The time of pain, diminishment, and recovery marks Ignatius's entry into his true self in God. Ignatius's new story begins here! Ignatius slowly, through the many months of recovery, begins to discover himself as beloved of God. It is from this excruciating experience of wounding that Ignatius vows his life to the following and service of Christ.

Aware of being loved by God changed everything. Ignatius went from warrior to servant!

Conversion and Transformation

Suggested approach to prayer: Suffering and Love

+ Daily prayer plan (Orientations xxxi)

I quiet myself and relax in the presence of God. I declare my dependency on God.

+ Grace: I beg for the gift of an intimate knowledge of the sharing of goods that God does in God's love for me. Filled with gratitude, I desire to love God and my neighbor "not only in word or in the experience of some tender moment of love but also…in deed and in truth…"

Method: Meditation (Orientations p.xxxiv)

"There are basically only two things needed for transformation: suffering and love. Everyone has this capacity. Hence, everybody is a possible subject for divine transformation." (Keating 2002, 51)

Encouraged by the statement of Father Keating, and after reading over the commentary of the conversions of St. Paul and St. Ignatius, reflect on your own life. Are there times, events, and circumstances of conversion in your life that mirror those of St. Paul and St. Ignatius?

+ List three times of significant growth and change in your life.

_____

_____

_____

+ For each of these times, recall the suffering that precipitated the change.

+ For each of these change-times, recall the people who supported and nurtured you.

+ How was God, through suffering and love, present and active during these times of conversion and transformation?

+ Have there been scripture passages that particularly influenced and nurtured your ongoing story of conversion and transformation? Recall and reread them.

+ As the time of your prayer draws to a conclusion, spend twenty minutes in quiet contemplative prayer.

+ Close your prayer with an Our Father.

+ Review of Prayer: Record in your journal the thoughts and feelings that have surfaced during your prayer.

Conversion and Transformation

Complimentary prayer: As Kingfishers Catch Fire

+ For this prayer period, use the introductory and closing frame-work of the previous prayer.

+ Method: Poetry as Prayer (Orientations p.xxxix)

+ Like St. Paul and St. Ignatius, as we discover ourselves as children of God, we welcome ourselves as unique, chosen, and loved by God. We discover who we are called to be and the mission to which we experience our inner selves called. We discover and live out of what John Duns Scotus called "our thisness." We do, indeed, put on the mind and heart of Christ.

+ In his poem, "As Kingfishers Catch Fire," Gerard Manley Hopkins explores this wondrous mystery: read and enjoy it.

As kingfishers catch fire, dragonflies draw flame;
As tumbled over rim in roundy wells
Stones ring; like each tucked string tells, each hung bell's
Bow sung finds tongue to fling out broad its name;
Each mortal thing does one thing and the same:
Deals out that being indoors each one dwells;
Selves- goes itself; *myself* it speaks and spells,
Crying *What I do is me: for that I came.*

I say more: the just man justices;
Keeps grace: that keeps all his goings graces;
Acts in God's eye what in God's eye he is—
Christ—for Christ plays in ten thousand places,
Lovely in limbs, and lovely in eyes not his
To the Father through the features of men's faces.

(*Poems and Prose* of Gerard Manley Hopkins)

Repetition Day: Love, always a mutual gifting, is proven in deeds more than words.

I quiet and relax in the presence of God.

Grace: I beg for the gift of an intimate knowledge of the sharing of goods that God does in his love for me. Filled with gratitude, I want to be empowered to respond just as totally in my love and service of God.

Approach to prayer: Repetition (Orientations p. xlii)

In preparation, I review my prayer by rereading my journal of the past days. I select for my repetition the period of prayer in which I was deeply moved by joy, gratitude, or awe. I proceed in the manner I did originally, focusing on the scene, word, or feeling that was previously most significant, or I may consider returning to a passage with which I experienced some difficulty.

Review of prayer: I write in my journal any feelings, experiences, or insights that have come to my awareness with a particular significance during this prayer period.

Point 2

God's Gifts to Me

God creates me out of love that desires nothing more than a return of love on my part. So much does God love me that even though I take myself away from him, God continues to be my Savior and Redeemer.

All my natural abilities and gifts, along with the gifts of Baptism and the Eucharist and the special graces lavished upon me, are only so many signs of how much God our Lord shares his life with me. My Consolation: who I am by the grace of God.

Spiritual Exercises, #234

THE GIFT OF LIFE

Ecclesiastics 17:1–13

> The Lord fashioned man [and woman] from the earth...
> He clothed them with strength like his own, and made them in his own image.
> He filled all living things with dread of man, making him master over beasts and birds. He shaped for them a mouth and tongue, eyes and ears, and gave them a heart to think with.
> He filled them with knowledge and understanding, and revealed to them good and evil. He put his own light in their hearts to show them the magnificence of his works.
> They will praise his holy name, as they tell of his magnificent works. He set knowledge before them; he endowed them with the law of life.
> He established an eternal covenant with them, and revealed his judgments to them. Their eyes saw his glorious majesty, and their ears heard the glory of his voice.

Commentary:

With the dawning of awareness, the first human beings stood on the crest of a hill and marveled at the world around them—the expanse of skies, the undulating hills, the rivers twisting among the trees. Perhaps the woman gasped in delight at the wild cries of the winged creatures who swept across the sky, and the inquisitive foxes that peered from behind a bush. This was life and it was beautiful! And the man may have looked into the bright eyes of his partner and rejoiced, even as he felt his own appreciation and thanksgiving rise up within him.

Life is a gift. And in the quiet of the night as they gazed into the sky and saw dancing movement of the flickering stars as they moved from season to season, they must have mused and wondered, and came to realize that, in spite of all the lurking dangers in their environment, the wonders of their world were gifts, gifts that pointed to a Giver.

From earliest times, human beings have pondered the mystery of life, what it is, from whence it comes. When the Hebrew people returned from Exile, they brought with them questions they had not pondered before about their God. They knew God as the God who gave a promise to Abraham, a God who drew them out of oppression into the freedom of their own land. Now they came to awareness, that not unlike the gods of Babylon, Yahweh was also a creator who had, indeed, created the world.

And they celebrated every aspect of creation in the great litany chanted in the newly built temple, a litany that became the first chapter of Genesis. "The spirit hovered over the chaos…God spoke…the sun, the moon, the earth…came into being…and it was good…and it was good" (Gen. 1).

Every people has pondered the gift of life. For the Lakota nation, life began after a great flood that destroyed all the people, except a beautiful young woman who, with the help of a big spotted eagle, Wanblee Galeshka, was saved and brought to the top of a tall tree that stood on the highest stone pinnacle in the Black

Hills. It was the one spot not covered with water. Eventually he made her his wife, for "there was a closer connection then between people and animals…" She gave birth to twins, a boy and a girl, whose children would become a great nation, the Lakota Oyate. And it was good (Lakota Creation Myth).

Today, those who embrace the recent scientific discoveries about the universe wrestle with the same questions of whence and who. It is suggested that if the book of Genesis were rewritten today, it might begin with something like this: "In the beginning was God, filled with power and mystery, and God spoke one Word, and the Word exploded into a tiny, hot, dense ball of matter that gave rise to forces and fields, quarks and particles, all joined together like a single strand of thread" (Delio 2008, 15).

Again, as we gaze into the heavens with the most powerful of telescopes, or ponder the microscopic world, our hearts are moved in wonder and thanksgiving.

In our hearts we ponder the mystery of love, that wonderful exchange of care, faithful, and tender that brings joy and light to our daily lives. And in pondering this mystery, human beings have discovered that the Creator, as fountain fullness, flowing into all of creation, is relational, never distant or static, but is continually creating and sustaining life. As people of God, we have always yearned for a way of speaking of the fullness of God's love. Theologically, this mystery of God's love has come to be expressed as Trinity, one God, yet three persons in a dynamic relationship of love. Although it is impossible for anyone to grasp the immensity of God's love, contemporary theologians and mystics are helping us, in a new way, to approach the mystery of the Trinity.

In the words of Elizabeth Johnson,

> A fresh insight into the lively character of this divine relationality comes from Western theology's rediscovery of the idea of *perichoresiss* (pronounced per-ee-kor-ee'-sis) to describe the inner life of God. Coined in Eastern theology, the Greek term describes a revolving around or cyclic movement like the revolution of a wheel. When applied to the life of the Trinity, this metaphor indicates that each of the "persons" dynamically moves around the others, interacts with the others, interweaves with the others in a circling of divine life. While remaining distinct, the three co-inhere in each other in a communion of love. (Johnson 2007, 213–214)

This communion of love can be likened to a dance, the Father loving the Son, the Son returning the love, and the love between the Father and the Son giving rise to the Spirit. God is at once, Lover, Loved, and Loving, or in the words of Hopkins, the "Utterer, Uttered and Uttering" (G. M. Hopkins, "Margaret Clitheroe," 79). God is Giver, Given, and Giving.

And we, made in the image and likeness of our God, know in the intimacy of loving and being loved, something of the Mystery that is our God. We are humbled before the awareness.

Into the future, this divinely choreographed dance goes on throughout all of creation as God draws all into the Trinitarian community in and through Christ and the Spirit.

Teilhard de Chardin speaks of this unfolding mystery as Christogenesis.

In the words of an ancient doxology, we pray: *Glory be to the Father, through the Son, and in the Holy Spirit.*

The Gift of Life

Suggested approach to prayer: Circle of Love

+ **Daily prayer plan** (Orientations p. xxxi)

I quiet myself and relax in the presence of God. I declare my dependency on God.

+ Grace: I beg for the gift of an intimate knowledge of the sharing that God does in his love for me. Filled with gratitude, I want to be empowered to respond just as totally in my love and service of God.

+ Method: Meditation (Orientations p.xxxiv)

> + In what relationships in your life do you experience the freedom of give-and-take as in a dance?

> + Consider the dynamic relationship of love within the Trinity, the giving and receiving of love between the Father, Son, and Spirit.

> —Image their relationship as a whirling dance, intimate and full of exuberant energy. How does contemplating their relationship as a dance influence or inspire you?

> —See yourself invited into the dance. Can you find your place?

—Who accompanies you in the dance? Is there anyone you leave out of your circle of dance? How do you see your dance of love mirroring that of the Trinity?

+ If so inclined, illustrate in some way this dance of love, perhaps using swirling colors, and the like.

+ Offer a prayer of thanksgiving for the Gift of so great a Creator.

+ At the close of your prayer time, spend twenty minutes in quiet contemplative prayer.

+ Close by praying an Our Father.

+ Review of Prayer: Record in your journal the thought and feelings that surfaced during your prayer.

Overflowing Abundance

Psalm 104

Bless Yahweh, my soul.
Yahweh my God, how great you are!
Clothed in majesty and glory, wrapped in a robe of light!

You stretched the heavens out like a tent,
you build your palace on the waters above;
using the clouds as your chariot,
you advance on the wings of the wind;
you use the wind as messengers, and fiery flames as servants.

You fixed the earth on its foundations,
unshakable for ever and ever;
you wrapped it with the deep as with a robe,
the waters overtopping the mountains.

At your reproof the waters took to flight,
they fled at the sound of your thunder,
cascading over the mountains, into the valleys,
down to the reservoir you made for them;
you impose the limits they must never cross again,
or they would once more flood the land.

You set springs gushing in ravines,
running down between the mountains,
supplying water for wild animals,

attracting the thirsty wild donkeys;
near there the birds of the air make their nests
and sing among the branches.

From your palace you water the uplands
until the ground has had all that your heavens have to
offer;
you make fresh grass grow for cattle
and those plants made use of by your people,
for them to get food for the soil:
wine to make them cheerful,
oil to make them happy
and bread to make them strong.

The trees of Yahweh get rain enough,
those cedars of Lebanon he planted;
here the little birds build their nest
and, at the highest branches, the stork has its home.
For the wild goats there are the mountains,
in the crags rock-badgers hide.

You made the moon to tell the seasons,
the sun knows when to set:
you bring darkness on, night falls,
all the forest animals come out:
savage lions roaring for their prey,
claiming their food from God.

The sun rises, they retire,
going back to lie down in their lairs,
and men and women go out to work, and to labor until dusk.
Yahweh, what variety you have created,
arranging everything so wisely!

Earth is completely full of things you have made:
among them vast expanse of oceans,
teeming with countless creatures, creatures large and
small,
with the ships going to and fro
and Leviathan whom you made to amuse you.

All creatures depend on you to feed them throughout the year;
you provide the food they eat,
with generous hand you satisfy their hunger.

You turn your face away, they suffer,
you stop their breath, they die and revert to dust.
You give breath, fresh life begins,
you keep renewing the earth.

Glory for ever to Yahweh!
May Yahweh find joy in what he creates,
at whose glance the earth trembles,
at whose touch the mountains smoke!

I mean to sing to Yahweh all my life,
I mean to play for my God as long as I live.
May these reflections of mine give him pleasure,
as much as Yahweh gives me!
May sinners banish from the earth
and the wicked exist no more!

Bless Yahweh, my soul.

Commentary:

Ask the cattle, who feeds you? Seek information from the birds: who provides a nesting place for you? And of the fishes of the sea: from where arise the waters in which you swim? Ask the trees, the mountains and the cascading rivers: from whence comes your beauty, your majesty and your power.

The creeping things of earth will give you lessons…There is not one such creature but will know this state of things is all of God's own making. God holds in power the soul of every living thing and the breath of each one's body. (Job 12:8–10)

Psalm 104 is a captivating feast for our imagination. We are enchanted as we are led by the psalmist through the vast array of creation. We breathe in the fragrance of the forests, we climb the mountains, we engage with each facet of God's loving gifts.

There are precious moments when one is suddenly aware of the mystery and majesty of creation.

One such moment came to St. Ignatius of Loyola early on in his life. In the first flush of his love for God, he spent time in prayer and in service in the town of Manresa. He later recalled that, one day, on the way to church, he found himself on a road next to the River Cardoner. He sat down for a while "with his face toward the river which was running deep." Suddenly "the eyes of his understanding began to be opened; though he did not see any vision, he understood and knew many things, both spiritual things and matters of faith and of learning, and this was with so great an enlightenment that everything seemed new to him." Years later he recalled this experience by the River Cardoner as a gift surpassing all the other helps he received from God through the years (Olin and O' Callaghan, 39–40).

The psalmist, like an artist, in beautiful and broad strokes, illustrates the profound lessons of the reality of God's creative love and the purpose of creation. So too, the mystic.

Fr. Cusson, SJ, says that

It is not false to say that Ignatius lived in a *divine milieu.*

Any small creature could put him into contact with God, because he unceasingly and concretely perceived that nothing exists or subsists without the active and loving presence of God, and that in return every creature becomes, in its own way, a reflection and proclamation of the divine grandeur. (Cusson 1988, 320–321)

Ignatius, in his direction and in his writing, always encouraged his followers to seek "God's presence in all things, in their conversations, their walks, in all that they see, taste, hear, understand, in all their actions, since His Divine Majesty is truly in all things by His presence, power, and essence" (Young 1959, 240). Ignatius wanted them, and us, to deeply realize that " all the things in this world are gifts of God, created for us, to be the means by which we can come to know God better, love God more surely, and serve God more faithfully."

Taking my place with and among all of creation—with the cattle, the birds, with the fishes, the mountains, the trees, the sun, and the stars—we sing:

Glory forever to Yahweh! May Yahweh find joy in what he creates! (Ps. 104:31)

Overflowing Abundance

Suggested approach to prayer: Greet and Bless

+ Daily prayer pattern (Orientations p. xxxi)

I quiet myself and relax in the presence of God. I declare my dependency on God.

+ Grace: I beg for the gift of an intimate knowledge of the sharing of goods that God does in love for me. Filled with gratitude, I want to be empowered to respond just as totally in my love and service of God.

+ Method: A Contemplative Walk

Slowly and prayerfully read and reread the psalm. You may choose to sing or read it aloud.

Let the images come alive in your imagination.
Underline the phrases/images that resonate within you. What are the memories from your own experience that surface?

What elements of creation would you like to add to the psalm? For example: a pet that has been a precious part of your life, a place to which you have traveled, a newly discovered planet, and so on.

Plan a time when you can take a leisurely walk. Be attentive to your surroundings: the canopy of the sky, the cloud formations, the trees, any animals that you may encounter. Be attentive to what engages your senses—-what you see, hear, smell, and the like. Thank God for the gift of each of your senses.

As you find yourself particularly attracted to something, pause, gaze on it. Let yourself enter within it and become one with it.

Let the exuberance and joy of the poet, a follower of Ignatius, be your own:

I kiss my hand
To the stars, lovely-asunder Starlight,
wafting him out of it; and
Glow, glory and thunder;
Kiss my hand to the dappled-with-damson west;
Since, tho' he is under the world's splendor and wonder,
His mystery must be instressed, stressed;
For I greet him the days I meet him,
and bless when I understand.
(G. M. Hopkins, SJ, "The Wreck of the Deutschland")

+ Toward the close of your prayer, spend twenty minutes in quiet contemplative prayer.

+ Close your prayer time with an Our Father.

+ Review of Prayer: Record in your journal the thoughts and feelings that surfaced during prayer.

Overflowing Abundance

Complimentary prayer: Te Deum

Your voice speaks:
Great God of my life, I will praise Thee on the three shores of Thy
one light.
I will plunge with my song into the sea of Thy glory:
    with rejoicing into the waves of Thy power.
Golden God of Thy stars, loud God of Thy storms,
    flaming God of Thy fire-spewing mountains,
God of Thy streams and of Thy seas, God of all beasts,
    God of all the cornfields and of wild roses,
I thank Thee for having awakened us, Lord,
    I thank Thee to the choirs of Thine angels.
Be praised for all that lives.

God of Thy Son, great God of Thine eternal compassion,
    great God of Thine erring humanity,
God of all them who suffer, God of all them who die,
    brotherly God on our dark spoor;
I thank Thee that Thou hast delivered us,
I thank Thee to the choirs of Thine angels.
Be praised for our blessedness!

God of Thine own Spirit, flooding in Thy depths from love to love,
    seething down into my soul,
Rushing through all my chambers, bringing fire to every heart,
Holy Creator or Thy new earth:
I thank Thee that I may thank Thee, Lord,

I thank Thee to the choirs of Thine angels.
God of my psalms, God of my harps, God of my organs and of
my mighty music,
    I will sing Thy praises on the three shores of Thy One Light.

I will plunge with my song into the sea of Thy glory:
    with shouts of joy into the waves of Thy power.
                    (G. von le Fort, *Hymns to the Church*, 51–52)

What Greater Gift

John 3:16

> God loved the world so much that he gave his only Son,
> so that everyone who believes in him may not be lost but
> may have eternal life.

Commentary:

Her eyes jaundiced, her tummy protruding with edema, her
breath coming in short gasps, the woman lay dying. She reached
out to place her frail hand on the head of her daughter who knelt
by the side of the bed. Her words came haltingly, but firmly. "You
are a beautiful young woman; you were such a beautiful baby.
Your Daddy and I love you, have always loved you. We wanted
you. We always wanted you."

Reaching beyond her own pain, the mother gave the reassurance
to her daughter who had never been certain that she was not an
"accident" or a "mistake." With that touch and those words, the
woman once again gave her daughter life, an assurance that was
a new beginning, a new story of being loved.

In the love of the mother, we catch a glimpse of the uncondi-
tional, self-emptying love of God, who has so loved us.

What mystery! God has given to the world his Son; God has giv-
en us a new story. Our God is an endlessly giving God. God is
the great giver gifting!

Throughout all of biblical history, God's loving generosity is evident.

When Abraham, the father of the Jewish people, was old and bereft of family and land, God looked upon him kindly and gave him his beloved son, Isaac. As God had promised, Abraham's descendants, the nation of Israel, became God's chosen people. They were the recipients of God's provident goodness, and God's great generosity to the Israelites is celebrated in the psalms of thanksgiving. We read how God saved the Israelites from the oppression of Egypt and brought them home and eventually brought them back from exile. "Happy the nation whose God is Yahweh, the people he has chosen for his heritage" (Ps. 33:12).

What greater gift could God have given to Abraham and Sarah than their son, Isaac? What greater gift could God have given to us than to give us his Son, Jesus Christ?

Scholars have come to recognize that the birth of Christ released into the universe an energy so powerful as to be compared to the big bang theory that initiated the birth of the universe. For those who believe, the energy of the incarnation changes and transforms everything.

The incarnation is

> ...a concentrated expression of divine love already poured out in creation...it links the transcendent God forever with the flesh of the cosmos. By becoming flesh, the Word acquires personal time, a life story, a death, and does so

as a participant in the history of the world. Matter itself now becomes a permanent reality of the Holy Mystery of God, who never shucks off this connection. (E. Johnson, "Deep Incarnation: Prepare for Astonishment" Lecture).

The people that walked in darkness have seen a great light;
On those who live in the land of deep shadow a light
has shown (Isa. 9:1). Jesus comes as radiant light to a world
shrouded in despair and doubt.

How do we receive God's gift? Can we find it within ourselves to embrace a truth beyond ourselves, beyond the shell of our woundedness? Will we choose to believe and to live in trust, to live in the light that is Christ? Can we order our life in this Light?

If we can say "yes" to this gift of God, then:

…radiant in his light we awaken as the Beloved…and everything that is hurt, everything that seemed to us dark, harsh, shameful, maimed, ugly, irreparably damaged, is in Him transformed. (St. Symeon, The New Theologian, from a collection of *Mystical Hymns*)

What Greater Gift

Suggested approach to prayer: Enduring Fragrance

+ Daily prayer plan (Orientations xxxi)

+ I quiet myself and relax in the presence of God.

+ I declare my dependency on God.

+ Grace: I beg for the gift of an intimate knowledge of the sharing of goods that God does in love for me. Filled with gratitude, I want to be empowered to respond just as totally in my love and service of God.

Method: A Meditative Reading (Orientations p. xxxviii)

In writing to the community of Corinth, Paul praises God who "makes us, in Christ, partners of his triumph, and through us is spreading the knowledge of himself, like a sweet smell, everywhere. We are Christ's incense to God...the sweet smell of life that leads to life" (2 Cor. 2:14–16).

Aware of the love that has been poured into each of us as beloved of the Father, and brothers and sisters of Christ, make your own the prayer of Blessed John Henry Cardinal Newman.

Radiating Christ

Lord Jesus Christ,
Help me to spread Your fragrance wherever I go.
Flood my soul with Your Spirit and Life.
Penetrate and possess my being so utterly
That my life may be a radiance of Yours.
Shine through me, and be so in me
That every soul I come in contact with
May feel Your Presence in my soul.
Let them look up and see no longer me but only Jesus.
Stay with me
And then I will begin to shine as You shine,
So to shine as to be a light for others.
The light, O Jesus, will be all from You.
None of it will be mine.
It will be You, shining on others through me.
Let me thus praise You
In the way in which You love best;
By shining on those around me.
Let me preach You without preaching,
Not by words but by example,
By the catching force,
The sympathetic influence of what I do,
The evident fullness of love
My heart bears for You. Amen.

+ Read this prayer like a love letter.

+ Highlight any phrases or words that especially touch you.

+ Consider memorizing the prayer.

+ At the close of your prayer, spend twenty minutes in quiet contemplative prayer.

+ Closing: Let your heart speak intimately with God. End with an Our Father.

+ Review of Prayer: Record in your journal the thoughts and feelings that surfaced during the prayer.

Remembering

Psalm 103

Bless Yahweh, my soul, bless his holy name, all that is in me!
Bless Yahweh, my soul, and remember all his kindnesses:

in forgiving all your offenses,
in curing all your diseases,
in redeeming your life from the Pit,
in crowning you with love and tenderness,
in filling your years with prosperity,
in renewing your youth like an eagle's.

Yahweh, who does what is right, is always on the side of the oppressed,
he reveals his intentions to Moses, his prowess to the sons of Israel.

Yahweh is tender and compassionate, slow to anger, most loving;
his indignation does not last forever,
his resentment exists a short time only;
he never treats us, never punishes us,
as our guilt and our sins deserve.

No less than the height of heaven over earth
is the greatness of his love for those who fear him;
he takes our sins farther away than the east is from the west.

As tenderly as a father treats his children,
so Yahweh treats those who fear him;
he knows what we are made of, he remembers we are dust.

We last no longer than grass, no longer than a wild flower
he Lives,
one gust of wind and we are gone, never to be seen
there again;

yet Yahweh for those who fear him lasts from all eternity
and forever,
like his goodness to their children's children,
as long as they keep his covenant and remember to obey
his precepts.

Yahweh has fixed his throne in the heavens, his empire is
over all.
Bless Yahweh, all his angels,
heroes mighty to enforce his word, attentive to his word
of command.

Bless Yahweh, all his armies, servants to enforce his will.
Bless Yahweh, all his creatures in every part of his empire!
Bless Yahweh, my soul.

Commentary:

It is a terrible thing to forget to remember. Yet we do.

How can we ever forget the gifts God has given us? How is it
that we get so mired in superficiality, in the distractions of our

culture? Why do we take for granted God's goodness to us? Is it that our level of consciousness is so dulled that we actually forget and neglect the gratitude that should arise from our utter dependency on God?

Please God, let us not forget! Let us remember; let us join with the psalmist in reiterating the myriad of gifts with which we are inundated. Let us, join in praise and thanksgiving!

In this Te Deum, a beautiful hymn of remembrance and praise, the psalmist, from his innermost heart, thanks God for the forgiveness of his sins, the healing of his illnesses, his rescue from death, and for God's promise to him of eternal life.

As children to a loving parent, we are totally indebted and dependent on God for our every need. From our beginning, in our mother's womb, God "knit us together." Like the psalmist, each of us in our inner heart can recall, how in spite of everything—poverty, rejection, illness, loss—God has continually and faithfully sustained us. Even when we turned away, God was with us, watching over us, protecting, and providing for us. At the time, we may have been carelessly unaware but retrospectively we see God's presence and care surrounding us. As the poet says:

> Someone I loved once gave me
> a box full of darkness.
>
> It took me years to understand
> That this, too, was a gift.
> (Oliver 2006, 52)

Also, we can think of all the natural abilities and gifts that each of us has received; our unique personality and talents, our particular history and family, our vocation and work, our strengths and weaknesses—all that we are. We remember the gift of our faith and the blessings of the sacraments, our initiation into faith through Baptism and God's continuing nurturance in Eucharist and the many other graces that have been graciously given to each of us.

Saints tell us that if the only prayer we utter is "Thank You," it would be enough.

Remembering

Suggested approach to prayer: With Gratitude

+ Daily prayer plan (Orientations p. xxxi)

I quiet myself and relax in the presence of God.

I declare my dependency on God.

+ Grace: I beg for the gift of an intimate knowledge of the sharing of goods that God does in love for me. Filled with gratitude, I want to be empowered to respond just as totally in my love and service of God.

Method: Meditation   (Orientations p.xxxiv)

Prayerfully reread Psalm 103, underlining those words or phrases that particularly touch you. What do they stir up within you?

Reflect on and list all the gifts of God in your own life.

Using your list, write your own psalm of thanksgiving and praise.

Bless Yahweh, my soul, bless his holy name, all that is in me!

Bless Yahweh, my soul and remember all his kindnesses.

At the end of writing your psalm, rest in the consciousness of how much God has loved you. In your own words, express your gratitude.

+ Review of prayer: Record in your journal the thoughts and feelings that surfaced during your prayer.

Remembering

Complimentary prayer: Who Am I?

+ In this prayer period, use the introduction and closing framework of the previous prayer.

+ Method: Poetry as Prayer (Orientations p. xxxix)

On March 4, 1946, imprisoned by the Nazis for his participation
in a plot to kill Hitler, Dietrich Bonhoeffer penned the following
poem. Prayerfully read it as a meditation on his interior struggle,
in the midst of degradation, to maintain his integrity, his faithfulness to God, and his heart's call.

Who Am I?

Who am I? They often tell me
I stepped from my cell's confinement
Calmly, cheerfully, firmly
Like a squire from his country-house.

Who am I? They often tell me
I used to speak to my wardens
Freely and friendly and clearly,
As though it were mine to command.

Who am I? They also tell me
I bore the days of misfortune
Equably, smilingly, proudly,
Like one accustomed to win.

Am I then really all that which other men tell of?
Or am I only what I myself know of myself?
Restless and longing and sick, like a bird in a cage,
Struggling for breath, as though hands were compressing
my throat
Yearning for colors, for flowers, for the voices of birds,
Thirsting for words of kindness, for neighborliness,
Tossing in expectations of great events,
Powerlessly trembling for friends at an infinite distance,

Weary and empty at praying, at thinking, at making,
Faint, and ready to say farewell to it all?

Who am I? This or the other?
Am I one person today and tomorrow another?
Am I both at once? A hypocrite before others.
And before myself a contemptibly woebegone weakling?
Or is something within me still like a beaten army,
Fleeing in disorder from victory, already achieved?
Who am I? They mock me, these lonely questions of mine.
Whoever I am, Thou knowest, O God, I am Thine!
(*Bonhoeffer*, 41)

+ Consider:

—As Bonhoeffer describes his yearnings, his thirsting, what do
we know of his life experiences, the memories that continue to
support him? How were they gifts of God to him?

—In the midst of the tension, the inner struggle, how does he come to rest?

—What do you imagine enabled him to claim the final, "Whoever I am, Thou knowest, O God, I am Thine"?

+ Prayerfully reflect on your own life.

—What are the experiences of your life that continue to shape and support you in times of struggle?

—For your own prayer, use, as a mantra, the words, "You know, O God, I am Yours."

Jacqueline Syrup Bergan and Marie Schwan, CSJ

Gift of Hope

1 Corinthians 1:4–9

> I never stop thanking God, for all the graces you have received through Jesus Christ. I thank him that you have been enriched in so many ways, especially in your teachers and preachers; the witness to Christ has indeed been strong among you so that you will not be without any of the gifts of the Spirit while you are waiting for our Lord Jesus Christ to be revealed; and he will keep you steady and without blame until the last day, the day of our Lord Jesus Christ, because God by calling you has joined you to his Son, Jesus Christ; and God is faithful.

Commentary:

A letter of hope! Paul is writing a letter of hope to those he loves.

He is writing to the people who made up the small Christian community in Corinth. It is obvious from the tone of the letter that Paul loves this community. Even though there were times when its members had driven him to tears, Paul praised their faith, their prayer, and their love and care for each other.

The people of this community experienced extremely difficult and rigorous life conditions: most of them were poor, some were slaves, and without exception all the people had suffered the effects of the immorality that characterized this port city.

The hope to which Paul is calling them is the realization that the gift of relationship they have received with Christ will remain with them to its fulfillment. Paul is telling them that with this gift they can trust God and even though they may at times falter, they will not be separated from the transforming love of God. Paul is saying, "in spite of the morally, dysfunctional environment in which you live and your own personals failings, God has been faithful to you, his people. God has enriched you in so many ways: he has blessed you with good leaders and teachers; and you, yourselves, have been given firm voices in which to share the Gospel. The community lacks no gift of the Spirit."

Paul never ceased thanking God for all the graces God has given to this beloved but fragile community of Corinth.

Our world is not so different from that of Paul's. Our communities today are also suffering the effect of an evil society. Daniel Berrigan tells us that "we are in the midst of awful obfuscation… the imperium is constantly multiplying both occasions and symbols of idolatry, whether in the summons to war or the enticements of appetite. More is better—more comforts, more money, more killing!" (Berrigan 1996, 31). It is indeed a dark time; it seems at times that we are more and more subject to the domination of excess and corruption. Watching the evening news can be absolutely heartbreaking.

War is constant. We are engaged in military conflicts that justify the use of robotic drone killings in which many innocent lives are sacrificed. In the name of national security, we justify assassination of "enemies" without providing them with their due judicial process. Many countries now have nuclear weapons or are striving to attain them. Peace is spoken of, even striven for, but leadership, mutual understanding, respect, and cooperation is found sorely lacking.

Our children continue to be raped, abused, and exploited. The leaders in whom we have placed our sacred trust have, in too many instances, betrayed that trust. Although some advance has been accomplished, women continue to be undervalued and exploited. In some countries, and especially during war, women and girls are mercilessly raped. In many cities, as well as rural areas, crime is rampant. In spite of efforts, guns are easily available to everyone, even, at times, to those among us who are mentally unstable.

Our economic stability has been eroded by corruption and greed causing suffering, unemployment, and poverty for many.

The list of woes and lamentations could continue!

It is a great sadness. Like the community of Corinth, we are desperate for a word of hope. Karl Barth suggests that as we reflect on our times, we need to "hold the Gospel in one hand, and the newspaper in the other" (Barth, source unknown).

When Paul encourages the early Christians to put their hope in a deep relationship with Christ, he is drawing on a long tradition of the Jewish community.

Over and again, the Jewish people found themselves in circumstances that were discouraging. And over again, God raised up prophets and spoke his assurance through them. And so we hear Jeremiah call the people to trust and to hope in God who assures them that "they will fight against you but shall not overcome you, for I am with you to deliver you—it is Yahweh who speaks" (Jer. 1:19). In the midst of Exile, when the people were far from their homeland, God reassures them and gives them hope through Ezekiel, "I am going to gather you together from all the foreign countries, and bring you home to your own land" (Ezek. 36:24).

In Isaiah, we see one who, not unlike Paul, is a messenger of hope for the people of his time. In Isaiah, we find a wondrous description of the God worthy of the trust of the people. In a vision, Isaiah sees the Lord whose "garments" fill the temple, fill the whole world. Isaiah hears the praise of the seraphim crying, "Holy, holy, holy is the Lord of hosts."

The message to Isaiah implies that the people "are not dependent on other kings or Sovereigns but on the overpowering and awesome effect of divine power" (Anderson 2007, 297).

Before such holiness, Isaiah can identify with his own lost and wayward people and cries out. The Lord who calls Isaiah is a gracious God, a God of compassion and forgiveness. God sends forgiveness and healing as a seraphim touches an ember taken from the altar to the lips of Isaiah.

When God asks, "Whom shall I send?" Isaiah, filled with the glory of God's compassionate presence, responds, "Send me."

Both St. Paul and the prophet Isaiah offer us the revelation of the incredible relationship with God that is ours through the mercy of God. Isaiah speaks of God; Paul speaks of Christ, the Word of God, who will heal us, empower, even in the midst of our broken and dysfunctional world, even in the midst of our own sinfulness, and offer us every reason to hope.

Gift of Hope

Suggested approach to prayer: Forgiven and Called

+ Daily prayer plan (Orientations xxxi)

+ I quiet myself and relax in the presence of God.

+ I declare my dependency on God.

+ Grace: I beg for the gift of an intimate knowledge of the sharing that God does in his love for me. Filled with gratitude, I want to be empowered to respond just as totally in my love and service of God.

+ Method: Meditation (Orientations xxxiv)

Read the letter from Paul as if it is addressed personally to you. Let the words speak directly to you. Hear Paul thank, praise, and reassure you.

Read the commentary especially noting the parallelism between the time of Isaiah, the time of Paul, and our own time. Be attentive to the message of hope, power, and forgiveness in both St. Paul and the Prophet Isaiah.

The Christian vocation is, in the eyes of Paul, a gracious summons by God "into relationship with his Son" (1 Cor. 1:9). And in Isaiah (6:1–2a, 3–8) we hear the strong call, "Whom shall I send?"

+ How do the gifts you have received call and strengthen you in your personal relationship with Christ?

+ Who have been the people in your life who have fostered and encouraged your relationship with Christ? For example, your parents, teachers, mentors, authors, and leaders.

+ When in the times you may have failed, have you become aware that God was still present, sustaining and enriching you?

+ When have you experienced the purification of healing, a fiery seraphim rushing to your aid?

+ Are you willing to enter a period of prayerful discernment to listen to the Spirit's movement within you, to seek clarification of how God is calling you and how, within the circumstances of your life, you are to respond?

+ As your time of your prayer draws to a conclusion, spend twenty minutes in quiet contemplative prayer.

+ Close your prayer with an Our Father.

+ Review of Prayer: Record in your journal the thoughts or feelings that have surfaced during your prayer.

Gift of Hope

Complimentary prayer: The Way It Is

+ In this prayer period, use the introductory and closing framework of the previous prayer.

+ Method: Poetry as Prayer (Orientations p.xxxix)

The poem "The Way It Is," by William Stafford, could serve as a way to express how we experience the constancy of the thread of hope in our lives. Prayerfully read the poem. Hear God call you to the promise and gift of hope.

There's a thread you follow. It goes among
things that change. But it doesn't change.
People wonder about what you are pursuing.
You have to explain about the thread.
But it is hard for others to see.
While you hold it you can't get lost,
Tragedies happen; people get hurt
or die; and you suffer and get old.
Nothing you do can stop time's unfolding.
You don't ever let go of the thread.
      (Stafford 1978, 42)

Gift of Hope

Complimentary prayer: Praying the Newspaper

+ In this prayer period, use the introductory and closing framework of the previous prayer.

+ Hold the daily newspaper in your hands, as if you were holding the planet. Ask for God's blessings on our broken, but still beautiful world.

+ Ask for the grace to see our world as Christ sees it, with compassion rather than cynicism, with sympathy and understanding rather than criticism. Let it be a way of expanding your heart.

+ Try to enter into the experience of the people who are reported on or imaged there. See them as Christ sees them; silently ask God's healing presence to be with them.

+ Trust that your own efforts as a Christian toward seeing and loving the world is also, somehow, a way of reaching out to others, and bringing into consciousness the gift of hope offered in the compassionate and healing presence of the Spirit of God.

Repetition Day: God is always gifting us.

Grace: I beg for the gift of an intimate knowledge of the sharing of goods that God does in his love for me. Filled with gratitude, I want to be empowered to respond just as totally in my love and service of God.

Approach to prayer: Repetition (Orientations p.xlii)

In preparation, I review my prayer by rereading my journal of the past days. I select for my repetition the period of prayer that most revealed to me the awareness of how totally God is always gifting me and all creation, and in which I was deeply moved by joy, gratitude, or awe. I proceed in the manner I did originally, focusing on the scene, word, or feeling that was previously most significant. I may choose to repeat a prayer period in which I had some difficulty.

I consider how, like any reasonable person, I am moved to respond to this God who has so gifted me. Moved by Love, I may find that I can best respond in the words of the following prayer of St. Ignatius:

> Take, Lord, and receive all my liberty, my memory, my understanding, and my entire will—all that I have and call my own. You have given it all to me. To you, Lord, I return it. Everything is yours: do with it what you will. Give me only your love and your grace. That is enough for me.

Review of prayer: I write in my journal any feelings, experiences, or insights that have come to my awareness with a particular significance during this prayer period.

Point 3

God's Gift of God's Self

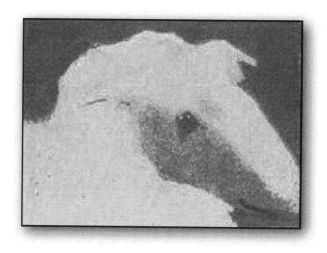

God not only gives gifts to me, but God literally gives himself to me. His is not only the Word in whom all things are created, but also the Word who becomes flesh and dwells with us. He gives himself to me so that his body and blood become the food and drink of my life. God pours out upon me the Spirit so that I can cry out "Abba." God loves me so much that I literally become a dwelling place or a temple of God—growing in an ever-deepening realization of the image and likeness of God which remains the glory of the creation of man and woman.

Spiritual Exercises: #235

Beauty's Self and Beauty's Giver

Wisdom 13:1–5

> Yes, naturally stupid are all men who have not known God and who, from the good things that are seen, have not been able to discover Him—who—is, or by studying the works, have failed to recognize the Artificer. Fire however, or wind, or the swift air, the sphere of the stars, impetuous water, heaven's lamps, are what they have held to be the gods who govern the world.
>
> If charmed by their beauty, they have taken things for gods, let them know how much the Lord of these excels them, since the very author of beauty has created them. And if they have been impressed by their power and energy, let them deduce from these how much mightier is he that has formed them, since through the grandeur and beauty of the creatures we may, by analogy, contemplate their Author.

Commentary:

"We walk in miracles like children scuff through daisy fields." (Eichner 1953)

It takes the eyes of a child—or a mystic—to recognize the miracle of God's presence in nature.

In the book of Wisdom, we find the invitation to discover God in the beauty, the magnificence of nature. Israel came to a knowledge of God, not through rational arguments, but through the saving acts of God on behalf of Israel.

While we find throughout the Old Testament praise for the power and majesty of the creating God, there was no mention of discovering God in the beauty of creation.

The author of Wisdom invites the reader to enter into the contemplation of all that is good and beautiful. While there are those who have looked upon fire, wind, the stars as Gods,

he says that they have failed to go beyond the beauty, they have not recognized the Artist, the Author, who not only created, but continues to shape them, and is present within them—if we have but eyes to see.

In his poem, "Pied Beauty," Gerard Manley Hopkins, SJ, has grasped and articulated the heart of this passage:

> Glory be to God for dappled things—
> For skies of couple-colour as a brinded cow;
> For rose-moles all in stipple upon trout that swim;
> Fresh-firecoal chestnut-falls; finches wings;
> Landscape plotted and pieced—fold, fallow, and plough;
> And all trades, their gear and tackle and trim.
> All things counter, original, spare, strange, stranger
> Whatever is fickle, freckled who knows how?
> With swift, slow; sweet, sour; adazzle, dim;
> He fathers-forth whose beauty is past change.
> (Hopkins:Gardner 1953, 30–31)

We are invited to:

Give beauty back, beauty, beauty, beauty, back to God,
beauty's self, and beauty's giver.
                    (Hopkins:Gardner 1953, 54)

Beauty's Self and Beauty's Giver

Suggest approach to prayer: For the Beauty of the Earth

+ Daily prayer plan: (Orientations p. xxxi)

+ I quiet myself and relax in the presence of God.

+ I declare my dependency on God.

+ Grace: I beg for the gift of an intimate knowledge of the sharing of good that God does in his love for me, and how God comes to me in each of his gifts. Filled with gratitude, I want to be empowered to respond just as totally in my love and service of God.

+ Method: Meditation (Orientations xxxiv)

Prayerfully read and reread the scripture passage. See it as a backdrop of your reflection as you let the words, and perhaps the music, of the following hymn, wash over your spirit, and become your prayer. Let the words elicit images that have been significant in your own life.

> For the beauty of the earth, for the glory of skies,
> For the love which form our birth, over and around us lies;
> Lord of
> all to you we raise, this our gift of grateful praise.

For the beauty of each hour, of the day and of the night,
Hill and vale, and tree and flower, sun and moon, and
stars of light: Lord
of all to you we raise, this our gift of grateful praise.

For the joy of human love, brother, sister, parent, child,
Friends on earth and friends above; for all gentle thoughts
and mild: Lord of
all to you we raise, this our gift of grateful praise.

For your Church, that evermore lifts its holy hands above,
offering up to every shore a pure sacrifice of love:
Lord of all to you we raise, this our gift of grateful praise.

For Yourself, O Gift Divine to our world so freely given,
For that love from which will shine, peace on earth and joy
in heaven: Lord
of all to you we raise, this our gift of grateful praise.

+ Toward the end of your time for prayer, spend twenty minutes
in quiet contemplative prayer.

+ Close your prayer with an Our Father.

+ Review of Prayer: Record in your journal the thoughts and feelings that surfaced during your prayer, especially any new awareness of how God has come to you through the gifts given to you.

To See with the Heart

Luke 2:1–8

> Now at this time Caesar Augustus issued a decree for a census of the whole world to be taken. This census—the first—took place while Quirinius was governor of Syria, and everyone went to his own town to be registered. So Joseph set out from the town of Nazareth in Galilee and traveled up to Judaea, to the town of David called Bethlehem, since he was of David's House and line, in order to be registered together with Mary, his betrothed, who was with child. While they were there the time came for her to have her child, and she gave birth to a son, her first-born. She wrapped him in swaddling clothes, and laid him in a manger because there was no room for them at the inn.

Commentary:

Mary holds her newborn child in her arms; she is enthralled as is any new mother. She is overwhelmed with tenderness for her small son. Even as she delights in her child, the words of the angel Gabriel arise within her heart, "the child will be holy and will be called the Son of God" (Luke 1:35). Mary ponders what these words might mean; she is aware that in the gift of God, God comes. She has said yes and she believes. Although the future is not clearly visible, her heart is open to the plan of God, a plan for the deliverance of her people.

Through the birth of Jesus, God visibly expresses his love for all of creation. In Christ, the identity of God is revealed in the created universe, which is, in turn, totally oriented to Christ. Christ is the goal of all created reality. To eyes that can see and hearts that are open, all of creation, the entire universe, sacramental as it is, participates in and reveals the living presence of the divine.

It is only with the heart that one can see rightly; what is essential is invisible to the eye. (de Saint Exupery 1971, 87)

In the familiar Christmas passage, Luke draws us into the universal significance of Christ's birth, the Incarnation. He sets the timeless event of Christ's birth in the historical context of the Roman census of the whole world. Christ comes for all humanity for all time. God comes "not as a stranger in the land," nor "like a traveler turning aside for the night" (Jer. 14:8). God, in Christ, has come to stay, to make his home among his people.

The humble manger in which the animals were fed is the place in which the newborn child is placed. The symbolism of the cave and the animals draws us into the birthing experience; it is within this primal place of the womblike cave and among the animals that God makes a definitive leap into creation.

Through the birth of Jesus, creation is given a decisive thrust toward God consciousness. We are given the power to become the children of God, to know our divine Source.

Think of the love that the Father has lavished on us,
by letting us be called God's children;
and that is what we are. (1 John 3:1)

We gaze upon the mother bent over her Child. With her, we are touched by the beauty of God shining in the eyes of this new-born child. What mystery!

When peaceful silence lay over all, and night had run the half of her swift course, down from the heavens, from the royal throne, leapt your all-powerful Word; into the heart of a doomed land...(Wisd. 18:14–15)

To See with the Heart

Suggested approach to prayer: In the Stable

In the Stable

+ Daily prayer plan (Orientations p.xxxi)

I quiet myself and relax in the presence of God. I declare my dependency on God.

+ Grace: I beg for the gift of an intimate knowledge of the sharing of goods that God does in his love for me, and how God comes to me through his gifts. Filled with gratitude, I want to be empowered to respond just as totally in my love and service of God.

+ Method: Ignatian Contemplation (Orientations xxxiv)

Prayerfully reread Luke 2:1–8.

Using the approach of Ignatian contemplation, set the scene of the Gospel of Christ's birth by imaging the stable in which Jesus will be born. Imagine the animals, the manger, the smells, the sounds, and the like.

Place yourself in the scene. Let your imaginative experience of the birth of Jesus unfold.

Can you imagine this scene in the center of your own being?

Open yourself, in stillness, to absorb the joy and amazement, the significance, of this holy event.

Stay with Mary and Joseph and offer joy, thanks, wonder, and praise for the great gift of God sharing himself in Christ.

+ Spend twenty minutes in contemplative prayer.

+ Close your prayer with an Our Father.

+ Review of prayer: Record in your journal the thoughts and feelings that surfaced during your prayer.

Kissed into Wholeness

Philippians 2:5–11

> In your mind you must be the same as Christ Jesus.
> Though in the form of God, Jesus did not claim equality
> with God but emptied himself, taking the form of a slave,
> human like one of us.
> Flesh and blood, he humbled himself, obeying to the
> death,
> death on a cross.
> For this very reason, God lifted him high and gave him
> the name
> above all names.
> So at the name of Jesus, every knee will bend in heaven,
> on earth, and in the world below,
> and every tongue exclaim to the glory of God the Father,
> "Jesus Christ is Lord."

Commentary:

Where do we most see God? If we have some appreciation of how, God's presence wondrously permeates all creation, how absolutely stunned we become when we contemplate that same presence of God permeating our own humanness and revealed in the dynamic of our genuine relationships with each other. "Finding God in all things means finding God's presence in rejection, betrayal, illness—the general craziness of life—as well as in great joy, faithful friends or good health" (Dyckman, Garvin, and Liebert 1989, 237).

How is it that we at arrive at this transforming vision of God's presence?

In your mind you must be the same as Christ Jesus. (Phil. 2:5)

The mind of Christ Jesus is revealed in the laying down of his life. This laying down of his life begins with "not claiming equality with God." In the self-emptying of all that would constitute clinging to God, Jesus embraces the vulnerability of all that is part of being human, "even death." Jesus surrenders the absolute security of the "state" of divinity in order to enter into the insecurity of being human. Jesus enters into the confusion, chaos, the suffering, and the joys that are the legacy of the human condition.

In becoming human, Jesus enters into a relationship of mutuality with all men and women for all time. He truly becomes our brother. In extending himself to others and in his relationships, Jesus models and makes visible the incredible outflowing energy of love that God has for all creation.

As Jesus continues to lay down his life in the service of his brothers and sisters, he opens the way for the Spirit's life and action to flow freely in the everyday exchanges they have with him and with each other.
As we enter more authentically into our own human relationships, that is, enter into the vulnerability of the daily give-and-take of loving, we, too, find ourselves laying down our lives, taking on the vision of the mind of Christ.

It is important to consider how one is to move toward the developing of authentic human relationships that reveal the presence of a loving God.

For Jesus, friendship is the foundation of relationships that are fully human. His friendships are characterized by the mutuality and equality that recognizes and affirms the dignity of each person. Each person in a friendship is raised up, becomes more than he or she ever dreamed. In our relationships we are called to "lay down our lives" for each other, to enter into the self-emptying love that is the hallmark of the love of Jesus.

Friendship is "the one human relationship based on equality." Jesus exemplifies this model. He shows us the beauty, joy, and healing gift that human friendship brings. In his instruction to his disciples, he clearly calls them to a depth of friendship, not only to himself but to each other, a commitment that may lead to death, itself. "I no longer call you servants, but friends" (John15:13-15). He is calling them, and us, to a radical new form of relationship. "If I, then, the Lord and Master, have washed your feet, you should wash each other's feet. I have given you an example so that you may copy what I have done to you" (John 13:12–15). He is calling us to a form of relationship that serves as our entry into joy. How happy and free the friendship in which the gift of self is seen and experienced as a deep-satisfying joy rather than some land of "sacrifice," diminishment, or impoverishment of self. "I have told you this so that my own joy may be in you and your joy may be complete. This is my commandment: love one another, as I have loved you" (John 15:11–12; Schneider 2003, 192–196).

There are, of course, relationships that are conditioned by the responsibility of one person for another. For example, parents *must* provide for the needs of their children. The relationship is one of inequality, the one person having what another needs. Based on domination, such a relationship can become abusive or oppressive as when a parent "uses" his or her child to fulfill his or her own needs or lives out personal dreams vicariously through the child or dependent person. The same could be true of a slave or servant to a master, or a poor person to a rich one.

Other relationships, like that of a teacher to a student, or a doctor to a patient, involve the freely offered gift of what one has to another who one perceives is in need of what one has. Again there is an inequality between the one who has and the one who has not.

These relationships can, though not necessarily, slip into domination or status seeking as when teachers use students to enhance their own status, or when doctors create dependency in patients, or when clergy treat their congregation as sheep to be led. "I tell you most solemnly, no servant is greater than his master, no messenger is greater than the one who sent him" (John 13:26; Schneider 2003.).

As followers of Jesus, we are asked to transform all our relationships so that they are transfused with the spirit of Jesus, a laying down of one's life for the other, a self-emptying that reveals the mind and heart of Jesus.

Empty yourself continually in honor of the Incarnate Word who emptied himself with so much love for you. Make your commitment to live in the practice of most sincere, true, and profound humility possible to you. Do so on all occasions, to everyone but especially to God, from whom must come all the blessings of your life. (J. P. Medaille, SJ)

In the joy of friendship, we discover the mind and heart of Christ Jesus. In the eyes of a friend, we catch a glimpse of the eyes and vision of Christ. Dare we enter into such happiness?

Aelred of Rievaulx, a twelfth-century teacher in the Celtic world, took as his ideal the relationship of love between Jesus and John. Aelred taught "that it is through one another that Christ kisses us into wholeness." There is, he says, the physical kiss, but then there is also "the spiritual kiss, the mingling of spirits, the merging of hearts in which we find that we are one" (Newell 2008, 85–86)

We thank God for those friends who lay down their lives for us, who in doing so reveal not only God shining in their eyes, but through whom, Christ kisses us into wholeness.

Kissed into Wholeness

Suggested approach to prayer: A Basin, Some Water, and a Towel

+ Daily prayer plan (Orientations p.xxxi)

I quiet myself and relax in the presence of God.
I declare my dependency on God.

Grace: I beg for the gift of an intimate knowledge of the sharing of goods that God does in his love for me, and how God comes to me in each of his gifts. Filled with gratitude, I want to be empowered to respond just as totally in my love and service of God.

+ Method: Ignatian Contemplation (Orientations p.xxxiv)

Prayerfully read the following passage from the Gospel of John.

> Now before the festival of the Passover, Jesus knew that his hour had come to depart from this world and go to the Father. Having loved his own who were in the world, he loved them to the end. The devil had already put it into the heart of Judas, son of Simon Iscariot, to betray him. And during supper Jesus, knowing that the Father had given all things into his hands, and that he had come from God and was going to God, got up from the table, took off his outer robe, and tied a towel around himself. Then he poured water into a basin and began to wash the disciples' feet and to wipe them with the towel that was tied around him. He came to Simon Peter, who said to him,

"Lord, are you going to wash my feet?" Jesus answered, "You do not know now what I am doing, but later you will understand." Peter said to him, "Lord, not my feet only but also my hands and my head!" Jesus said to him, "One who has bathed does not need to wash, except for the feet, but is entirely clean. And you are clean, though not all of you." For he knew who was to betray him; for this reason he said, "Not all of you are clean."

After he had washed their feet, had put on his robe and had returned to the table, he said to them, "Do you know what I have done to you? You call me Teacher and Lord— and you are right, for that is what I am. So if I, your Lord and Teacher, have washed your feet, you also ought to wash one another's feet. For I have set you an example, that you also should do as I have done to you. Very truly, I tell you, servants are not greater than their master, nor are messengers greater than the one who sent them." (John 13:1–16)

+ Using your imagination, employing all your senses, enter into a contemplation of the passage.

I imagine Jesus walking into my church on a Sunday morning. I see him open his hands to all of us gathered. He speaks to us in a way that deeply touches our hearts. "I have not called you servants, but friends."

I am aware of what passes through my mind, what surges within me, when I hear him say these words.

I see Jesus look over the congregation. He calls forth a number of people. I hear him call the names of several others, and I see their response, how they rise reluctantly or eagerly.

I hear him call my name and see him look at me lovingly and humbly. I take care to experience within myself both of these attitudes of Christ as he looks at me.

I see Jesus gather those he has specially called. He invites us to be seated in the sanctuary. Then deliberately and lovingly, he brings a basin of water and some towels. He disrobes and stands before us, stripped except for a loincloth.

I notice the shadow of scars on his side, on his hands, and on his feet. Jesus kneels before me and begins to wash my feet. I am acutely aware of my feelings, perhaps of embarrassment or wonder and awe or tenderness.

When Jesus has finished, he says to me, "As I have done for you, go and do likewise for the others."

I stay with the washing of the feet allowing the experience to deepen within me.

At the close of the formal contemplation, I consider:

How am I being called to "wash the feet of others"? To whom will I go?

How will the intimacy and love of Jesus for me spill over into my family, into anyone I encounter? Is there someone whom I, for some reason, am resistant to expressing love, that is, a lack of willingness to wash his/her feet?

How am I being called, in what special way, to minister to my fellow Christians in my faith community? Do I have special gifts or skills that I might offer to my parish?

How am I being called to service in the community in which I live and work? What are the feelings or fears that seem to hold me back? I intentionally consider how I am being called to "wash the feet" of the poor and disadvantaged, those who may be suffering the injustices of abuse or neglect.

I engage in a heartfelt conversation with Christ. I let it be a prayer of personal friendship, expressing my hopes, my needs, my love, and gratitude. I especially ask that Christ would empower me in service to all I meet.

+ As the time of your prayer draws to a conclusion, spend twenty minutes in quiet contemplative prayer.

+ Close your prayer with an Our Father.

+ Review of Prayer: Record in your journal the thoughts and feeling that surfaced during your prayer.

Kissed into Wholeness

Complimentary prayer: Into the Unknown

+ In this prayer period, use the introductory and closing framework of the previous prayer.

+ Method: Poetry as Prayer (Orientations p.xxxix)

Prayerfully read and reread the following poem by T. S. Eliot.

> In order to arrive there,
> To arrive where you are, to get from where you are not,
> You must go by a way wherein there is no ecstasy.
> In order to arrive at what you do not know
> You must go by a way which is the way of ignorance.
> In order to possess what you do not possess
> You must go by the way of dispossession.
> In order to arrive at what you are not
> You must go through the way in which you are not.
> And what you do not know is the only thing you know
> And what you own is what you do not own
> And where you are is where you are not.
> (T. S. Eliot, "East Coker")

+ How does this poem resonate with the concept of Jesus becoming human, emptying himself even to the point of laying down his life? Can you see this poem in the context of the Incarnation?

+ To what does this poem call you to in your relationship with others?

+ Look at a friendship in which you experience mutuality and equality.

Recall the history of that relationship. How has it been an experience of self-emptying?

How has it brought about in you a radical shift from fantasy to the reality of entering into the unfamiliar, the not knowing, not having all the answers?

How has your experience of this genuine relationship carried you from the immaturity of control and self-doubt to the living out of a complete dependency on God and an enduring faith in the Spirit's presence and action?

+ How do the commentary, Eliot's poem, and your experience of authentic friendship integrate the words of Paul as he addresses the community of Philippi?

+ How is every authentic relationship a step into the unknown, calling for a radical self-emptying?

Light in the Darkness

2 Corinthians 4:5–10

> For it is not ourselves that we are preaching, but Christ Jesus as the Lord, and ourselves as your servants for Jesus' sake. It is the same God that said, "Let there be light shining out of darkness," who has shown in our minds to radiate the light of the knowledge of God's glory, the glory on the face of Christ.
>
> We are only the earthenware jars that hold this treasure, to make it clear that such an overwhelming power comes from God and not from us. We are in difficulties on all sides, but never cornered; we see no answer to our problems, but never despair; we have been persecuted, but never deserted; knocked down, but never killed; always, wherever we may be, we carry with us in our body the death of Jesus, so that the life of Jesus, too, may always be seen in our bodies.

Commentary:

He awoke in the night and lay listening. He couldn't remember where he was. The thought made him smile. Where are we? He said

> *What is it, Papa?*
>
> *Nothing. We're okay. Go to sleep.*

We're going to be okay, arent we Papa?

Yes. We are.

And nothing bad is going to happen to us.

That's right.

Because we're carrying the fire.

Yes. Because we're carrying the fire. (McCarthy 2006, 83)

Taken from the post-apocalyptic Pulitzer Prize novel *The Road*, by Cormac McCarthy, this is the dialogue between a father and his young son as they walk the roads together toward the sea. They are survivors in a world that has been totally devastated. They journey alone through burned America; nothing moves in the ravished landscape except the acrid ash on the wind. Everything is gray. There is no sound of birds or leaves in the wind. All is covered with ash and smells of death. They have only a pistol to protect themselves against the bands of savage ruthless marauders, and a cart of scavenged food—and each other. They carry a lit lantern.

In some ways this dialogue echoes the spirit if not the words of Paul to the people in Corinth. They, too, were living in a time of oppression and persecution. The Christian community that Paul established in Corinth was composed mostly of poor people. Given that the populous city of Corinth was a notorious center of immorality, it was a milieu that could create awkward situations and conflictual problems to those newly converted to Christ. Like the father and son in the dialogue above, the early Christians of Corinth were a minority, threatened by forces beyond their control; all they had was each other and the light of their faith in an unknown future.

Against this backdrop of "difficulties on all sides," Paul offers reassurance to the fledgling community of Corinth. However newly birthed and fragile they may experience themselves to be, Paul reminds them that it is the same God that said "Let there be light shining out of darkness" who dwells in and empowers them as they proceed forward on their faith journey. Paul encourages them saying, that it will not only be "okay" but assures them that their experience of the death of Jesus is a necessary prelude to their experience of the risen life of Jesus within them.

In offering encouragement, Paul is instructing the community on the necessity and transforming power of suffering. Through the pain of suffering, each one will arrive at a point in which he or she must encounter his or her own inner darkness. This encounter is essential in order that they will be empowered and open to letting go of whatever they previously thought was essential to their idea of happiness. In this dying to self, the baptized Christian will, in their own humanness, in some mysterious way, participate in the death of Jesus. In their newfound freedom, they will experience the life and light of Jesus radiating within them and through them.

Individually and collectively, the people of the community of Corinth are like earthenware jars, fragile and flawed. And yet, they carry within them incredible treasure, the fire, and the light of the risen Christ, whom they are called to bring to others.

In the poignant conclusion of *The Road*, we see the father who knowing that he is dying, offers words of encouragement and support to his son who understandably is seized with fear and doubt.

I want to be with you.

You cant.

Please.

You cant. You have to carry the fire.

I dont know how to

Yes you do.

Is it real? The fire?

Yes it is.

Where is it? I dont know where it is.

Yes you do. It's inside you. It was always there. I can see it.

Just take me with you. Please.
I cant.

Please, Papa.

I cant.

You said you wouldnt ever leave me.

I know. I'm sorry. You have my whole heart. You always did. You're the best guy. You always were. If I am not here you can still talk to me. You can talk to me and I will talk to you. You'll see. (McCarthy 2006, 269–270)

Light in the Darkness

Suggested approach to prayer: Carrying the Fire

+ Daily prayer plan (Orientations xxxi)

I quiet myself and relax in the presence of God.

I declare my dependency on God.

Grace: I beg for the gift of an intimate knowledge of the sharing of goods that God does in his love for me, and how God comes to me in each of his gifts. Filled with gratitude, I want to be empowered to respond just as totally in my love and service of God.

Method: Ignatian Contemplation (Orientations xxxiv)

You have been on a journey down the road of your life. Write a brief description of or draw an image of your road. See yourself on the road.

You have carried a unique fire within you.

How has the fire been contained within you and how has it been sustained? Describe your fire to another person.

Do you claim and love your fire?

In which ways does your fire radiate and bring light to others?

Savor the words of Teilhard de Chardin, SJ

> Throughout my whole life during every moment I have lived, the world has been gradually taking on light and fire for me, until it has come to envelop me in one mass of luminosity, glowing from within...
>
> (Teilhard de Chardin, 1960, 13)

+ Spend twenty minutes in quiet contemplative prayer.

+ Close your prayer with an Our Father.

+ Review of Prayer: Record in your journal the thoughts and feelings that surfaced during your prayer.

Giver and Gift

Luke 22:19

Do this in remembrance of me.

Commentary:

Someday after mastering winds, waves, tides and gravity, we shall harness the energies of love, and then, for the second time in the history of the world, we will discover fire. (Teilhard de Chardin)

We stand on the threshold of that "someday."

Contemporary science is revealing integrative connections and dynamic possibilities that were never previously scientifically substantiated but, mysteriously, were always present within the deepest levels of our yearning. We are being presented with the fruits of scientific research and scholarship that call us to a radical shift of consciousness. These discoveries are altering and challenging our fundamental ways of thinking of ourselves and our relationships with each other and our universe. We are being thrust forth into an entirely new paradigm, a new mode of self-organization, which has the power to release the profound depth of identity that the mystics and poets have intuitively known.

Simultaneously, over the past decades, we have seen the emergence of a new theological perspective that articulates the need for a relevant theology for our times. Theologians have begun to incorporate the new insights of science in a creative process that enhances, and impels forward, the biblical and doctrinal traditions that have sustained us throughout past centuries.

The mystic knows that we have long been prepared for this new time.

The most radical shift the world has known is the Incarnation, "the definitive event in Christianity in which divine life spilled over into human life in the person of Jesus of Nazareth" (Cannato 2006, 71).

The fire of God's love in Christ was made visible in the life of Jesus. God's love was manifested in Jesus's words, acts, and in signs. We see one of the greatest signs of God's love as we contemplate Jesus at his Last Supper. In Eucharist, God gifts us and in the gifting God gives himself. God is giver and gift.

At the Last Supper as Jesus gathered with his disciples for the Passover meal, they experienced anew the incredible love that Jesus had for them. The power of his love would set them on fire with zeal and impel them to the ends of the earth.

On the threshold of his death, Jesus took bread, blessed, broke, shared it, and said, "do this in remembrance of me." He took the cup of wine and blessed it, saying, "This is the cup of the covenant of my blood shed for you. Take and drink." Each time they break bread and share wine, they will know his presence.

Jesus has invited the disciples to go forth and do as he has done, to be as he is. Jesus is responding to the deepest desires in their hearts. They will be bread broken and shared; they will pour out their lives in loving service. For the disciples and for us, in the intimate and simple act of sharing bread and wine, God continues to draw us into union with him and each other. The Last Supper illustrates the revolutionary shift that the incarnation represents.

Nothing will ever be the same.

The evolutionary imperative of our time is relational. Beatrice Bruteau succinctly expresses this in the following way:

> The view of the sacred world that I am proposing says that the world consists of communication—interactions among its components or members in which they exchange matter, energy, and information. I feel that we should recognize and celebrate it as a gigantic Eucharist in which one sees all the others with each ones own being. (Bruteau 1997, 13–14)

Jesus invites the disciples *to be* Eucharist. Their call is our call. In them and through us, the world will discover, day by day, one by one, the "fire" of love.

Giver and Gift

Suggested approach to prayer: The Greatest Mark

+ Daily prayer pattern (Orientations xxxi)

I quiet myself and relax in the presence of God.

I declare my dependency on God.

+ Grace: I beg for the gift of an intimate knowledge of the sharing of goods that God does in his love for me and how God comes to me in each of his gifts. Filled with gratitude, I want to be empowered to respond just as totally in my love and service of God.

+ Method: Ignatian Contemplation (Orientations p. xxxiv)

St. Ignatius calls the giving of the Eucharist "the greatest mark of Jesus' love."

Imagine yourself invited to be present at the Last Supper. See yourself making your way through the city streets of Jerusalem, anticipating the celebration of the Passover meal with Jesus and his closest followers.

Walk up the steps leading to the Upper Room. As you enter, see the vaulted ceiling reflected in the lamps that are set out on the table. Let your eyes be drawn to the table laid out with cups of wine, loaves of bread, and the small bowls of bitter herbs. Be aware of the warm and tantalizing smell of the lamb roasting in the adjoining room. Find a place at the table and be aware as the disciples enter into the room and take their places. Listen to their conversations and feel free to join them. Finally see Jesus as he enters the room, pauses to look around, and acknowledge each person there, then takes his place.

Prayerfully, slowly, read the following, pausing to let each phrase come to life for you. Allow each of your senses to help create the experience. Be aware of the feelings and movements of your heart as you see and hear Jesus's words.

When the hour came he took his place at table, and the apostles with him.

And he said to them, "I have longed to eat this passover with you before I suffer; because I tell you, I shall not eat it again until it is fulfilled in the kingdom of God."

Then, taking a cup, he gave thanks and said, "Take this and share it among you, because from now on, I tell you, I shall not drink wine until the kingdom of God comes."

Then he took some bread, and when he had given thanks, broke it and gave it to them saying, "This is my body which will be given for you; do this as a memorial of me."

He did the same with the cup after supper, and said, "This cup is the new covenant in my blood which will be poured out for you." (Luke 22:14–20)

Consider how, as Jesus approaches the final moments of his life, he can do no more, can give no greater gift, how the memorial gift of his Body and Blood is placed into the hands and hearts of those who love and follow him.

Let your heart respond.

+ Toward the close of your prayer, spend twenty minutes in contemplative prayer.

+ Close your prayer with an Our Father.

+ Review of prayer: Record in your journal the thoughts and feelings that surfaced during your prayer.

Giver and Gift

Complimentary prayer: Mass on the World

+ In this prayer period use the introductory and closing framework of the previous prayer.

+ Method: Meditation (Orientations p.xxxiv)

On a bleak morning, in the mountains of central China, Teilhard de Chardin found himself alone and unable to offer mass. In the coming of the new day, as he contemplated his surroundings, his heart overflowed with the following prayer:

> Over there on the horizon, the sun has just touched with light the outermost fringe of the eastern sky

> Once again, beneath this moving sheet of fire, the living surface of the earth wakes and trembles, and once again begins his fearful travail.

> I will place on my paten, O God, the harvest to be won by this renewal of labor.

> Into my chalice I shall pour all the sap which is to be pressed out this day from the earth's fruits.

> My paten and my chalice are the depths of a soul laid widely open to all the forces which in a moment will

rise up from every corner of the earth and converge upon the Spirit…

Receive, O Lord, this all embracing host which your whole creation,
moved by your magnetism, offers you at this dawn of a new day.

(de Chardin 1961, 19–20)

Imagine yourself standing with Teilhard. Enter into and make your own, his prayer and his offering.

Giver and Gift

Complimentary prayer: The Darkness Is Deep

In this prayer period, use the introductory and closing framework of the previous prayer.

+ Method: Poetry as Prayer (Orientations p. xxxix)

A Ritual to Read to Each Other

If you don't know the kind of person I am
and I don't know the kind of person you are
a pattern that others made may prevail in the world
and following the wrong god home we may miss our star.

For there is many a small betrayal in the mind,
a shrug that lets the fragile sequence break
sending with shouts the horrible errors of childhood
storming out to play through the broken dike.

And as elephants parade holding each elephant's tail,
but if one wanders the circus won't find the park,
I call it cruel and maybe the root of all cruelty
to know what occurs but not recognize the fact.

And so I appeal to a voice, to something shadowy,
a remote important region in all who talk:
though we could fool each other, we should consider less
the parade of our mutual life get lost in the dark.

For it is important that awake people be awake,
Or a breaking line may discourage them back to
sleep: the signals we give—yes, or no or maybe—
should be clear: the darkness around us is deep.

(W. Stafford 1993, 135)

Giver and Gift

Complimentary prayer: The Eucharist and Our Daily Lives

+ In this prayer period, use the introductory and closing framework of the previous prayer.

+ Method: Meditation (Orientations p.xxxiv)

Come, Lord, enter my heart,
you who are crucified, who have died, who love,
who are faithful, truthful, patient, and humble,
you who have taken upon yourself a slow and toilsome life
in a single comer of the world,
denied by those who are your own,
too little loved by your friends,
betrayed by them, subjected to the law,
made the plaything of politics right from the very first,
a refugee child, a carpenter's son, a creature who found
only barrenness and futility as a result of his labors,
a man who loved and who found no love in response,
you who were too exalted for those about you to understand,
you who were left desolate,
who were brought to the point of feeling yourself forsaken by God,
you who sacrificed all, who commend yourself into the hands of
your Father,
you who cry: "My God, my Father, why have your forsaken me?"

I will receive you as you are,
make you the inner most law of my life,

take you as at once the burden and the strength of my life.
When I receive you I accept my everyday just as it is.
I do not need to have any lofty feelings in my heart to recount
to you.
I can lay my every day before you just as it is,
for I receive it from you yourself,
the everyday and its inward light,
the everyday and its meaning,
the everyday and the power to endure it,
the sheer familiarity of it
which becomes the dimmedness of your eternal life.

(Rahner, SJ 1965, 62)

All about Jesus

Luke 9:28–36

> Now about eight days after this had been said, he took with him Peter and John and James and went up the mountain to pray. As he prayed, the aspect of his face was changed and his clothing became brilliant as lightning. Suddenly there were two men there talking to him; they were Moses and Elijah appearing in glory, and they were speaking of his passing that he was to accomplish in Jerusalem. Peter and his companions were heavy with sleep, but they kept awake and saw his glory and the two men standing with him. As these were leaving him, Peter said to Jesus, "Master, it is wonderful for us to be here; so let us make three tents, one for you, one for Moses and one for Elijah." He did not know what he was saying. As he spoke, a cloud came and covered them with shadow; and when they went into the cloud, the disciples were afraid. And a voice came from the cloud saying, "This is my Son, the Chosen One. Listen to him." And after the voice had spoken, Jesus was found alone. The disciples kept silence and, at that time, told no one what they had seen.

Jesus—it is all about Jesus!

Jesus is the center. Brilliantly, Jesus is revealed. All else falls away!

In this moment in the life of Jesus, as he is in prayer, his face and entire demeanor become luminous. The inner essence and identity of Jesus radiantly shine forth in glorious light. He is transfigured.

The disciples who accompanied him witness this incredible transformation. In the man who led them up the mountain, they now see a fullness they could not possibly have imagined. Suddenly, the veil of their past history and experience is lifted. They see Moses and Elijah in conversation with Jesus and their ancestral story is enlightened. The Moses and Elijah of their cultural inheritance have led to his moment, this person, Jesus. They recognize that all the richness of the Law and the Prophets are now reappropriated in Jesus. In this moment, as they see Jesus transparent in glory, they know deeply the covenantal promise that is being revealed in him. As if for the first time, they see Jesus, and see him for who he is, Son of God, the Chosen One.

In the glory of Jesus transformed, the disciples see themselves as invited into the unfolding mystery of Jesus. This new awareness impels them to reflect deeply on the life of Jesus and to "listen" to his teaching. This new consciousness will prompt them to let go of whatever might hinder his life and light within them; they will see with new eyes.

> What the mystic seeks is not an appearance of God in the world, but a shining of God through his creation, a "diaphany" of God shining through the transparent world. This Christ, shining diaphanously through every creature of the universe, is encountered in a loving act of surrender in which Christ becomes the "Thou" complementing our "I." Each Christian now awakened to a new consciousness

of Christ's universal presence discovers his or her own self-realization and full maturity in "being-with-Christ." Christ becomes the unifying and integrating center in creation, as each person seeks his or herself in Christ and thus in one another. (Delio 2008, 80)

What we see in the Transfiguration of Jesus is the potential of the realization of the dream of all humanity, of all creation. We hold in our hearts the dream of fullness and completion that can only be realized by the placing of Christ as the center of our hearts.

The transfiguration story suggests that, like the disciples, we may one day suddenly realize we are in the presence of Christ. Whether we find Christ in the broken people around us, the beauty of creation, the struggle for justice and peace, the suffering of the poor, the love of our enemies, or the breaking of the bread, we will recognize the light of Christ shining in our midst…we will understand ourselves as children of the Light, servants of the Light, and instruments of the Light. We will feel the love, forgiveness, and compassion of the transfigured Christ enlightening us. We will reject the world's darkness, with all its violence, fear, hostility, and wars, and find new hope, purpose and meaning in his light. Suddenly we will be disarmed and feel the peace of the transfigured risen Christ. Without having to undergo a near-death experience, we too will want to spend the rest of our lives seeking his light, sharing his light, and living in his light. From now on, we will always want to dwell in the light of the transfigured Christ. (Dear 2007, 87)

All about Jesus

Suggested approach to prayer: Radiant Light

+ Daily prayer plan (Orientations p.xxxi)

I quiet myself and relax in the presence of God. I declare my dependency on God.

+ Grace:

I beg for the gift of an intimate knowledge of the sharing of goods that God does in his love for me, and how God comes to me in each of his gifts. Filled with gratitude, I want to be empowered to respond just as totally in my love and service of God.

Method: Ignatian Contemplation (Orientations p.xxxiv)

Sit comfortably on a chair or on the floor. Feel the breath moving in and out of your body and sense your body relaxing as you slowing inhale and exhale.

Reread the passage.

I see myself with Peter, James, and John. We have reached the summit. We watch as Jesus draws away a short distance from us.

I contemplate Jesus as he enters into prayer with God. I become aware of how the union of love with his Father is reflected in the serenity of his face, the quiet confidence of his total demeanor.

Suddenly, it is as if Jesus is enveloped in light, a radiance that transforms him. His face and clothing become luminous.

In your imagination, gaze on the light as it encircles Jesus at prayer. Open yourself to receive the light radiating in rays from him as it flows from him to you.

Pay attention to the gentle movement of the light. Feel yourself becoming one with the light. Maintain your focus on Jesus.

As you open your heart, sense the light within you. See it radiate through your body, transversing its path throughout your entire body. The light embraces every part of you so that you, in turn, are filled and radiant with the light of Jesus.

Return to the awareness of your breath. As you inhale, breathe in the light of Christ. As you exhale, let go of anything that hinders the light. Continue in this practice, resting in his light and presence.

In the deep recesses of your heart, listen to Jesus, "I am the light of the world; anyone who follows me will not be walking in the dark; he/she will have the light of life" (John 8:12).

Read and savor the words of John Dear, SJ:

> The transfiguration story suggests that, like the disciples, we may one day suddenly realize we are in the presence

of Christ. Whether we find Christ in the broken people around us, the beauty of creation, the struggle for justice and peace, the suffering of the poor, the love of our enemies, or the breaking of the bread, we will recognize the light of Christ shining in our midst…we will understand ourselves as children of the Light, servants of the Light, and instruments of the Light. We will feel the love, forgiveness, and compassion of the transfigured Christ enlightening us. We will reject the world's darkness, with all its violence, fear, hostility, and wars, and find new hope, purpose and meaning in his light. Suddenly we will be disarmed and feel the peace of the transfigured risen Christ. Without having to undergo a near-death experience, we too will want to spend the rest of our lives seeking his light, sharing his light, and living in his light. From now on, we will always want to dwell in the light of the transfigured Christ. (Dear 2007, 87)

+ At the close of your prayer, spend twenty minutes in quiet contemplative prayer.

+ Close your prayer time with an Our Father.

+ Review of Prayer: Record in my journal the thoughts and feelings that surfaced during your prayer.

All about Jesus

Complimentary prayer: Every Branch Afire

+ In this prayer period, use the introductory and closing framework of the previous prayer.

+ Method: Poetry as Prayer (Orientations p.xxxix)

Let the somewhat whimsical poem by Elizabeth Browning invite your reflection.

Earth is crammed with heaven.
And every branch afire with God;
But only he who sees, takes off his shoes,
The rest sit around it, and pick blackberries.

Repetition Day: God dwells in and comes to us his Gifts.

Grace: I beg for the gift of an intimate knowledge of the sharing of goods that God does in his love for me, and how God comes to me through each of his gifts. Filled with gratitude, I want to be empowered to respond just as totally in my love and service of God.

Approach to prayer: Repetition (Orientations p. xlii)

In preparation, I review my prayer by rereading my journal of the past days. I select for my repetition the period of prayer that most revealed to me an awareness of how God is present and comes to us in and through his gifts, and in which I was deeply moved by joy, amazement, gratitude, or awe. I proceed in the manner I did originally, focusing on the scene, word, feeling, or passage that was previously most significant. I may choose to return to a passage with which I had difficulty.
I consider how, like any reasonable person, I am moved to respond to this God who comes to me through the many gifts of creation. Moved by love, I may find that I can best respond in the words of the following prayer of St. Ignatius:

> Take, Lord, and receive all my liberty, my memory, my understanding, and my entire will-all that I have and call my own. You have given it all to me. To you, Lord, I return it. Everything is yours; do with it what you will. Give me only your love and your grace. That is enough for me.

Review of prayer: I write in my journal any feelings, experiences, or insights that have come to my awareness with a particular significance during this prayer period.

Point 4

God Labors to Share his Life and Love

God loves me so much that God enters into the very struggle of life. Like a potter with clay, like a mother in childbirth, or like a mighty force blowing life into dead bones, God labors to share his life and love. God's labors take him even to death on a cross in order to bring forth the life of the Resurrection.

Spiritual Exercises, #236

GOD LABORS

John 5:17

My Father goes on working, and so do I.

Commentary:

"That God works, that he labors in all things, that he struggles when the galaxies move, that the rush of all life is indicative of his sacred toil, that all things are caught up in the repetitive workings of God" (Stanley 1986, 302) reveals how intimately God is present and active in all of life. In whatever circumstances we may find ourselves, we can trust that God will be actively present as when the prophet Hosea says,

> When Israel was a child I loved him, and I called my son out of
> Egypt But the more I called to them, the further they went from me;
> they have offered sacrifice to the Baals...
> I myself taught Ephraim to walk, I took them in my arms;
> yet they have not understood that I was the one looking after them. I led them with reins of kindness with leading-strings of love.
> I was like someone who lifts an infant close against his cheek;
> stooping down to him I gave him his food. (Hosea 11:1–4)

"My Father goes on working and so do I." With these words Jesus claims a God who is neither distant nor static but rather a

Father, who is very much like a mother, who is completely engaged with all he has created. Jesus claims a Father whose faithful, tender kindness knows no bounds, whose love overflows freely, disciplining those he loves with gracious generosity. The work of the Father is present in the ongoing action of creating, nurturing, healing, and restoring life.

As a true son of his Father, Jesus does what the Father does. He heals; he feeds; he restores life. On the Sabbath, standing before and among his neighbors in the synagogue, Jesus claimed as his own the words of the prophet, Isaiah:

> The spirit of the Lord has been given to me, for he has anointed me.
> He has sent me to bring the good news to the poor,
> to proclaim liberty to captives and to the blind new sight,
> to set the downtrodden free, to proclaim the Lord's year of favor. (Luke 4:18)

Jesus heals the sick, he feeds those who are hungry, he calms those who are frightened, he challenges those who have lost their way. "My Father goes on working and so do I."

The God of Jesus is the God of history. Throughout all Hebraic history, we see God as always faithful, tenderly kind, and everlasting. At the beginning of Israel's history, God reassured Abraham, "I will be your God and you will be my people." He is the God of promise. When enslaved in Egypt and in the experience of the Exodus, the Israelites came to know God, "I am Yahweh your God who brought you out of the land of Egypt, out of the house of slavery" (Exod. 20:2). In their enslavement, oppression, hunger, and homelessness, as they trekked through the desert wastelands, God was with them.

> Remember how Yahweh your God led you for forty years in the wilderness, to humble you, to test you and know your inmost heart—whether you keep his commandments or not. He humbled you, he made you feel hunger, he fed you with manna…to make you understand that we do not live on bread alone but we live on everything that comes from the mouth of Yahweh. The clothes on your back did not wear out and your feet were not swollen, all those forty years. (Deut. 8:1–14)

How awesome this God of Israel! Yet as their history unfolded over the next centuries, the Israelites, under pressure, seemed to have had a poor memory of their God of faithful compassion. Repeatedly, they broke their covenant with God, yet God, ever faithful, repeatedly drew them back and renewed his covenant with them.

We see Israel at a low ebb when Jesus begins his public ministry. Religious practice had deteriorated into an oppressive legalism strangling the spirit of the people. It had become a religion of elitism; only those with the leisure to create the 613 laws would know the law, therefore be in a position to practice the minute and burdensome stipulations. The poor were at a distinct disadvantage; not knowing the law, it was impossible to follow the law. There were labeled as sinners and treated as unclean.

Jesus challenged the harsh legalism when on the Sabbath, at the pool of Bethzatha, he healed a man who had been sick for thirty-eight years, "Get up, pick up your sleeping mat and walk." The Pharisees who were always looking for infractions of the law promptly criticized him for violating their interpretation of what it meant to keep holy the Sabbath. Jesus responded asking them if they would not do as much for an animal. He asked them if a donkey falls into a pit on the Sabbath do they not rescue it.

The Pharisees are further disturbed when Jesus identifies himself with God by saying "My Father is always working and so am I." Jesus reminded them that the Rabbis already held that God cannot rest on the Sabbath since God must continually hold in existence all that is. The love of God that Jesus embodies is not circumscribed by time and the excessive constraints of legalism.

Jesus, in all his words and actions, brings alive the reality of his Father's presence here and now.

Suggested approach to prayer: Anointed and Sent

+ Daily prayer plan (Orientations p. xxxi)

I quiet myself and relax in the
presence of God. I declare my
dependency on God.

Grace: I beg for the gift of an intimate knowledge of the sharing of goods that God does in his love for me, and in particular
how God labors and enters into the struggles of life. Filled with
gratitude, I want to be empowered to respond just as totally in
my love and service of God.

Method: Meditation (Orientations p. xxxiv)

> The spirit of the Lord Yahweh has been
> given to me, for Yahweh has anointed me.
> He has sent me to bring good news
> to the poor, to bind up hearts that are broken;
> to proclaim liberty to captives, freedom to those in prison;
> to proclaim a year of favor from Yahweh...
> to comfort all those who mourn and to give them for ashes
> a garland;
> for mourning robe, the oil of gladness, for despondency,
> praise.
>
> (Isa. 61:1–3a)

Read and reread this beautiful passage from Isaiah. Allow the
words to enter deeply within you.

Take each line of the passage and allow to surface the experiences in your own life that parallel the words and images in that particular line.

Where do find your heart most resonating?

Contemplate how, in Jesus, God labored and continues to work through Jesus on your behalf.

Compose your own prayer or psalm of gratitude. In your writing be attentive to the name(s) by which you address God.

+ As the time of your prayer draws to a conclusion, spend twenty minutes in quiet contemplative prayer.

+ Close your prayer time with an Our Father.

+ Review of Prayer: Record in your journal the thoughts and feelings that have surfaced during your prayer.

Complimentary prayer: Jesus's Work of Healing

+ In this prayer period, use the introductory and closing framework of the previous prayer.

Prayerfully read the following passage in St. Mark's Gospel. Be attentive to the actions and words of Jesus as he enters into the labor of healing the paralyzed man.

> When he returned to Capernaum some time later, word went round that he was back; and so many people collected that there was no room left, even in front of the door. He was preaching the word to them when some people came bringing him a paralytic carried by four men, but as the crowd made it impossible to get the man to him, they stripped the roof over the place where Jesus was; and when they had made an opening, they lowered the stretcher on which the paralytic lay. Seeing their faith, Jesus said to the paralytic, "My child, your sins are forgiven." Now some scribes were sitting there, and they thought to themselves, "How can this man talk like that? He is blaspheming. Who can forgive sins but God?" Jesus, inwardly aware that this was what they were thinking, said to them, "Why do you have these thoughts in your hearts?" Which of these is easier; to say to the paralytic, "Your sins are forgiven" or to say, "Get up, pick up your stretcher and walk"? But to prove to you that the Son of Man has authority on earth to forgive sins— he said to the paralytic—"I order you: get up, pick up your stretcher, and go off home." And the man got up,

picked up his stretcher at once and walked out in front of everyone, so that they were all astounded and praised God saying, "We have never seen anything like this."

(Mark 2:1–12)

+ As you read the passage attentively, note the many details of conversations and actions.

+ Using your imagination, employing all your senses, create the scene.

What kind of day is it? Is it hot or cold? Is it early morning or late in the day?
Do you feel a breeze on your skin? Are you aware of the texture of your clothing?
Are there fragrances in the air or perhaps smells of cooking?
What do you hear? Is the crowd noisy or subdued?
What most attracts your vision? Is it Jesus or the crowd on which you are most focused? Do you recognize any of the people, either those in the crowd or those carrying the stretcher?

+ Take your place in the scene. You might see yourself as a person in the crowd or one of the people carrying the stretcher or you could choose to be the paralytic.

+ Listen to the voices. How do the voices of the crowd sound? Are they hostile, arrogant, full of surprise, and the like? How does the voice of Jesus sound? Does his voice express anger, disbelief, compassion, and so on?

+ Imagine Jesus looking at you. What is his expression? Does he see a place within you that is blocked, perhaps a hidden area of "paralysis"?

+ What does Jesus say to you?

+ Continue praying in this way, being present and imaginatively taking your part in this event of Jesus healing the paralyzed person.

+ When you feel you are ready, offer your words of gratitude and praise for God's continued laboring in bringing forth the fullness of life within you.

Taming the Clay

Jeremiah 18:1–6

> The word to Jeremiah by Yahweh was, "Get up and make your way down to the potter's house; there I shall let you hear what I have to say." So I went down to the potter's house; and there he was, working at the wheel. And whenever the vessel he was making came out wrong, as happens with clay handled by potters, he would start afresh and work it into another vessel, as potters do. Then this word of Yahweh was addressed to me, "House of Israel, can I not do to you what this potter does?—it is Yahweh who speaks.
>
> Yes, as the clay is in the potter's hand, so you are in mine, House of Israel."

Commentary:

The wheel used by the potter was actually two stones or wooden discs set one upon the other, the top one pivoting on the lower one. The work of the wheel required great skill and coordination. As the potter molded the clay on the upper disc, he rotated the lower disc with his foot. It was a full person effort and called for intense focus and concentration. Becoming a true craftsman was a lifelong task.

Not only was it hard and demanding work, but it required patience and persistence. Many things could go awry. Many factors can distort a vessel on the wheel, such as the wrong constituency of clay, any foreign substance in the clay, improper treading, or lack of skill in treading or throwing the pot. To throw a pot may, at first sight, look simple but the making of a clay object on a wheel is more complex than meets the eye. The encouraging feature is that inherent in the clay is a myriad of possibilities; the potter simply breaks down the unacceptable creation, rolls it into a ball and begins again. In the mutual yielding and resistance between the clay and the potter, a new creation appears. With the reworking of the clay, with its particular texture, color, and consistency, the clay is "in formed" by the vision of the potter and becomes a unique vessel appropriate to its particular function. Creativity is always unpredictable, surprising, never static.

Jeremiah uses the image of the potter and the clay to symbolize the relationship between Yahweh and Israel. The prophet Jeremiah lived through the tragic years before and after the fall of the Kingdom of Judah. After a brief period of raised hopes, the death of the king of Judah upset the Mideastern balance of power. As a result violence erupted and intense suffering ensued. Eventually Jerusalem was captured, its temple burned, and many of its inhabitants deported. Desperate and discouraged, the people questioned the presence of their God, Yahweh. "Ruin on ruin is the news; the whole land is made waste, my tents are suddenly destroyed, in one moment all that shelters me is gone... Why has Yahweh our God done all of this to us?" (Jer. 4:20, 5:19).

Jeremiah experienced the anguish of the people in his own soul. "Of an affectionate and gentle disposition, he was nevertheless called, 'to tear up and to knock down, to destroy and to overthrow'…" (Introduction to the Prophets, Jerusalem Bible, 1126). Even under the political pressures, he endured and maintained the primacy of things of the spirit and an awareness of the intimacy required in relationship with God. He embodied all that was best in the Judaic tradition.

Having received the vision of the potter and the clay, Jeremiah hears a further instruction, "So now, say this to the people of Judah and the citizens of Jerusalem, 'Yahweh says this: Listen, I have been preparing a disaster for you, I have been working out a plan against you. So now, each one of you, turn back from your evil ways, amend your conduct and actions'" (Jer. 18:11).

Jeremiah offers hope to his people by calling them to radical remembrance and repentance.

The story of the potter and the clay is our story; it speaks strongly, individually, and collectively, to the breakdown and collapse of structures in which we have placed our trust. We are in great need of hearing the urgent message of the prophet Jeremiah. We need to hear his promise of hope, we need to hear again that God will bring life out of our dismal situation. In spite of everything, in the midst of all the chaos, loss, fear, and dysfunction, our Creator God will shape in us a newness, will bring to life the dream that lives within us. Jeremiah summons us to remember our creative God. We have been snagged into the slough of forgetfulness; in the forgetting of our God lies the danger of our corruption. Jeremiah says we must remember. Our future, individually and collectively depends on this remembering.

To remember…is not simply the calling up of something of the past, but a calling to mind, a state of retaining something in one's awareness. We are reminded to remember by the One who instilled remembrance in us… Our remembrance is His remembering…Remembrance of God is establishing a relationship with infinite Being, which is both nearer to ourselves and, at the same time, greater than anything we can conceive. It is also experienced as loving and being loved by love.

(Helminski 2002, 97, 100)

How great is the love of the Potter for the clay!

Is Ephraim, then, so dear a son to me, a child so favored that after each threat of mine I must still remember him, still be deeply moved for him, and let my tenderness yearn over him? It is Yahweh who speaks. (Jer. 31:20)

In the remembrance is the repentance. With each memory of God's creating love, we are restored. A new fresh and integrative way of being and living emerges, a new morality. We become more conscious of the whole and how everything we do affects the whole and as our conscience is awakened, not only our personality is altered but we become more sensitive in our relationships.

We live, move, and breathe more contemplatively. We are gentled and tamed. Our interactions with each other and our environment become more authentically transparent of our relationship with

God. This new consciousness is the only secure basis for genuine systemic change as our planet faces the future. Hope lives in our hearts. The past and the future are permeated with remembering God, a remembering that allows us to see the face of God within our present reality. At times "the veil between the earthly and the Divine become very thin (Helminski 2002, 102).

> Lo! as the potter mouldeth plastic clay
> To form his varying fancy doth display
> So in Thy hand, O God of love, are we. (Quoted in Anchor Bible, Jeremiah, 818)

Taming the Clay

Suggested approach to prayer: Shaped from Within

+ Daily prayer plan (Orientations xxxi)

I quiet myself and relax in the presence of God. I declare my dependency on God.

Grace: I beg for the gift of an intimate knowledge of the sharing of goods that God does in his love for me, and in particular how God labors and enters into the struggle of life. Filled with gratitude, I want to be empowered to respond just as totally in my Love and service of God.

Method: Ignatian Contemplation   (Orientations p.xxxiv)

+ Prayerfully reread the passage.

+ See yourself in the potter's shed. See the shelves that hold pots that are in various stages of completion. Some are large; some small. Some are decorative; some are for a practical use.

+ Let your eyes focus on the potter as he carefully chooses the clay. Carefully, he holds it in big hands, gently massaging it. Then, he slices through it to remove any lumps or foreign particles. Eventually he places it on the wheel and begins to form it.

+ Consider yourself as clay in the hands of the Potter. What kind of clay are you? Dry and stiff, or moist and yielding to the touch of the Potter.

+ Bring your thinking mind down into your heart; submerge it in the heart space and allow a deep receptivity to the presence of God within. Nurture a sense of the energy of God working within you, supporting, and shaping you.

+ Rest in yielding to the power and presence of God.

As the time of your prayer draws to a conclusion, spend twenty minutes in quiet contemplative prayer.

+ Close your prayer with an Our Father.

+ Review of Prayer: Record in your journal the thoughts and feelings that have surfaced during your prayer.

Taming the Clay

Complimentary prayer: Remembering

In this prayer period, use the introductory and closing framework of the previous prayer.

+ Method: Meditation   (Orientations p. xxxiv)

+ Enter again into the image of yourself as clay in the hands of the Divine Potter.

+ Consider how God has been shaping and reshaping you throughout your life.

In each phase of your life, recall events—joyful and painful. Recall persons who were significant during different phases of your life. Reflect how through each event and how through each person God has been at work within you, through the breakdowns and the breakthroughs that have been part of bringing you to this moment in time.

Before your birth.

During your childhood.

During your adolescence.

In your early maturity.

In the time since.

+ As you remember each precious moment of your life, enter into the awareness of how, in your remembering, God is also remembering, re-membering you.

"Truly in God's remembering, hearts find peace." (Helminski 2002, 100)

Let your heart be grateful.

Birth through Chaos

Romans 8:18–23

> I think that what we suffer in this life can never be compared to the glory, as yet unrevealed, which is waiting for us. The whole creation is eagerly waiting for God to reveal his sons. It was not for any fault on the part of creation that it was made unable to attain its purpose, it was made so by God; but creation still retains the hope of being freed, like us, from its slavery to decadence, to enjoy the same freedom and glory as the children of God. From the beginning till now the entire creation, as we know, has been groaning in one act of giving birth; and not only creation, but all of us who possess the first fruits of the Spirit, we too groan inwardly as we wait for our bodies to be set free.

Commentary:

"The world is dear. It is dear to God as God's Child, and it should be dear to us" (Bruteau 1997, 43).

The fire of divine love holds everything in existence; it energizes and propels the entire world, and indeed the entire cosmos, forward. This divine love transforms everything through its love energy. In the first moment of creation, in the outpouring of God's love—Christ is first in God's intention to love. Christ embodies the creative love of God and in him all creation finds its purpose. Penetrated with love all creation becomes luminous.

"Christ is the fire 'bursting' into the cosmic milieu to 'amorize' it, that is, to energize it in love" (Delio 2008, 74).

This insight, so dear to mystics, was already present in the writings of St. Paul. In this passage from Romans, Paul reminds his fellow Christians that although suffering is a part and sign of the following of Christ, the suffering will lead to glory, to the fullness of life. Earth, he sees, also shares in the experience of death issuing into life. He draws on the thought of the Greek philosophers who often compared the spring rebirth of nature to a woman's birth pains. It, they, we, even in our sufferings, groan in hope and expectation.

Paradoxically, in the midst of the breakdowns, collapse, and the accompanying experience of powerlessness that characterize our particular time in history, we are being gifted and freed by the Spirit with an exponential awareness and grasp of the dynamic of God's continual action in creation. This heightened awareness of God's regenerating presence moves us from an image of the universe as static and fixed, to one that is unfolding and immensely large in both time and space. God continues to give birth and is actively engaged into bringing Creation to its fullness in Christ. Christ is the model and pattern for the fulfillment of the universe as it reaches toward its Omega point.

> As a woman with child near her
> time writhes and cries out in her
> pangs, so are we, Yahweh, in your
> presence: we have conceived, we
> writhe as if we were giving birth. (Isa. 26:17)

There is no birth without pain. The birth process is very stressful as wave after wave of contracting pain is endured by the mother. The moment the baby passes through the birth canal is a critically dangerous time. The baby is suddenly thrust from the secure confinement of its mother's womb; it must rapidly inhale or suffer serious consequences, possibly even die. The baby takes its first breath. New life has emerged!

The birth of life is a paradigm for the incredible shifts of consciousness our world situation is demanding. The caution is not to succumb to the fear, anxiety, and panic that attends major change. The temptation is to grasp for control and to return to structures and systems that once gave security. To reactively grasp what has been is to regress, decline, and eventually die. There is no option but to make our way through the treacherous canal of birth. This birth can be gentled through trust in the slow unfolding of life and the energy of God's love shaping and molding a new way of being.

> God create a clean heart in me, put into me a new
> and constant spirit...(Ps. 51:10)

The newborn infant enters a whole new world very different from the totally contained and safe environ of his mother. So it is with us. The new consciousness that is challenging us and into which we are finding ourselves thrust, with accelerated speed, is both chaotic and exhilarating. We are on the threshold of new forms of thought, relationships, and the emergence of new structures. In the midst of this tumultuous time, we must not forget that it is the Divine Presence that is empowering this great change.

For now I create new heavens and a new earth, and the past will not be remembered, and will come no more to men's minds. Be glad and rejoice for ever and ever for what I am creating, because I now create Jerusalem "Joy" and her people "Gladness." (Isa. 66:17–19)

Birth through Chaos

Suggested approach to prayer: Patient Trust

+ Daily prayer plan (Orientations p. xxxi)

I quiet myself and relax in the presence of God. I declare my dependency on God.

Grace: I beg for the gift of an intimate knowledge of the sharing of goods that God does in his love for me, and in particular how God labors and enters into the struggles of life. Filled with gratitude, I want to be empowered just as totally in my love and service of God.

Method: Meditation (Orientations p.xxxiv)

+ In the context of the scripture passage and commentary, read, admire, and appreciate the wisdom of Pierre Teilhard de Chardin, SJ, a paleontologist, and mystic, who died in 1955.

> Above all, trust in the slow work of God.
> We are quite naturally impatient in everything to reach the end
> without delay. We should like to skip the intermediate stages.
> We are impatient of being on the way to something unknown,
> something new.

And yet it is the law of all progress that it is made by
passing through
some stages of instability—and that it may take a very
long time.
And so I think it is with you.
Your ideas mature gradually—let them grow, let them shape
themselves,
without undue haste.
Don't try to force them on, as though you could be today
what time
will make of you tomorrow.
Only God could say what this new spirit gradually forming
within
you will be. Give our Lord the benefit of believing that his
hand is
leading you,
and accept the anxiety of feeling yourself in suspense and
incomplete.

(de Chardin 1961, 57)

Claim and rest with what resonates within you.

+ As the time of your prayer draws to a conclusion, spend twenty
minutes in quiet contemplative prayer.

+ Close your prayer time with an Our Father.

+ Review of Prayer: Record in your journal the thoughts and feeling that have surfaced during your prayer.

Beside the Streams of Babylon

Ezekiel 37:1–14

The hand of Yahweh was laid on me, and he carried me away by the spirit of Yahweh and set me down in the middle of a valley, a valley full of bones. He made me walk up and down among them. There were vast quantities of these bones on the ground the whole length of the valley; and they were quite dried up. He said to me, "Son of man, can these bones live?" I said, "You know, Lord Yahweh." He said, "Prophesy over these bones. Say, 'Dry bones, hear the word of Yahweh. The Lord Yahweh says this to these bones: I am now going to make the breath enter you, and you will live. I shall put sinews on you, I shall make flesh grow on you, I shall cover you with skin and give you breath, and you will live; and you will learn that I am Yahweh.' I prophesied as I had been ordered. While I was prophesying, there was a noise, a sound of clattering, and the bones joined together. I looked and saw that they were covered with sinews; flesh was growing on them and skin was covering them, but there was no breath in them. He said to me, "Prophesy to the breath; prophesy, son of man. Say to the breath, 'The Lord Yahweh says this: Come from the four winds, breath; breathe on these dead; let them live!'" I prophesied as he had ordered me, and the breath entered them; they came to life again and stood up on their feet, a great, an immense army.

Then he said, "Son of man, these bones are the whole House of Israel. They keep saying, ' Our bones are dried up, our hope has gone; we are as good as dead.' So prophesy. Say to them, 'The Lord Yahweh says this: I am now going to open your graves; I mean to raise you from your graves, my people, and lead you back to the soil of Israel. And you will know that I am Yahweh, when I open your graves and raise you from your graves, my people. And I shall put my spirit in you, and you will live and I shall resettle you on your own soil; and you will know that I, Yahweh, have said and done this—it is the Lord Yahweh who speaks.'"

Commentary:

Once again, the breath of God moves over the chaos (Gen. 1:2).

This finely crafted and beautifully rendered metaphorical image of the restoration of the dead bones portrays a God of promise, a God who continually restores and in-spirits his people. This prophesy from Ezekiel is rightfully the most celebrated of all his oracles.

Written in the sixth century BC and addressed to the Jewish people in Exile in Babylon, it has been the subject of Rabbinic study, been incorporated into Christian liturgy, and has been the theme of countless hymns and spirituals. Its voice speaks as strongly and urgently to us as it did to those of the sixth century BC. The Israelites in exile were restored to life; we, in chaos, await that same creative breath.

The image of the field of dry and disparate bones expresses the hopelessness of the Israelite people. The drastic death and burial metaphors of Ezekiel serve as a perfect vehicle for the despondency and hopelessness of the Israelites. They were displaced from their homeland and had lost their temple, their king, and their connectedness to all they held dear. They experienced a depth of cultural and religious collapse of such insurmountable magnitude it could only be described as death. They recognized in the vision of the dead, dry, and scattered bones their own situation.

Does their strife foreshadow our own? "...human life on earth may now stand at a major transitional point, comparable perhaps to the fall of the great civilizations of the past... " (Needleman 2009, 29).

What does the vision of Ezekiel have to say to us? Dare we face the dead bones of our own cultural collapse through which we daily walk? Can we see in the disconnectedness, the abuse, poverty, corporate greed, homelessness, terrorism, and endless wars of our times the bones of a deteriorated and desperate people?

Beside the streams of Babylon we sat and wept... (Ps. 137:1)

As we sit beside our polluted rivers, we cry out "Where is *our* God?"

Once again, the breath of God moves over the chaos.

The Lord Yahweh says this to these bones; I am now to make the breath enter you and you will live. (Ezek. 37:5)

Like the powerful wind of Pentecost, God intervenes and remembers his people, breathing into them new life. It is at the seemingly greatest crisis points that a new thing breaks forth. New structures and new ways of connecting emerge from all directions. In the breath of God's own Spirit, people are gathered together and brought home to themselves and their God.

Instill some joy and gladness in me,
let the bones you have crushed rejoice again. (Ps. 51:8)

Beside the Streams of Babylon

Suggested approaches to prayer: Breath of Hope

+ Daily prayer plan (Orientations p.xxxi)

I quiet myself and relax in the presence of God.

I declare my dependency on God.

Grace: I beg for the grace of an intimate knowledge of the sharing of goods that God does in his love of me in particular how God labors and enters into the struggle of life. Filled, with gratitude, I want to be empowered just as totally in my love and service of God.

Method: Meditation   (Orientations p.xxxiv)

Unite yourself with God. See yourself one with God as he lovingly gazes upon the earth.

Take and reverently hold a globe of the planet in your hands. Look at the globe, and see where fresh life is emerging: fields of grain, reforestation projects, peace initiatives, renewal of structures and families, research and discovery of energy sources, and the like.

As you turn the globe in your hands, be aware of those places that are fields of dead bones; places where war is being waged, the intense suffering of throngs of displaced refuges, where lands are being devastated by the ravages of climate change and the earth's resources exploited, the threatened extinction of precious species. Be aware of city streets where crime, hunger, and pollution threaten the quality of life, and so on.

Breathe in the pain of the planet and allow it to penetrate your heart. Breathe out healing, tender kindness, and peace. When you envision the joy of newness in our planet, breathe it out, send it out with the wish that everyone, everywhere would experience the hope of a new beginning.

It is in the kinship with the pain and joy of each other, that the breath of God regenerates and restores the people of the earth.

In the spirit of Father Arrupe, pray:

> Loving God, with that voice that you make groan in the depths of my being I seek the copious pouring out of Your-self, like the rain that gives back life to the arid earth, and like a breath of life that comes to animate dry bones. Give me that Spirit that scrutinizes all, inspires all, teaches all, that will strengthen me to support what I am not able to support.
>
> Give me that Spirit that transformed the weak Galilean fishermen into the columns of your Church and into Apostles who gave in the holocaust of their lives the supreme testimony of their love for their brother and sisters.
>
> (Arrupe 1979, 296–297)

Let your heart sing an alleluia for both the pain and the joy.

> Alleluia!
> Praise Yahweh, my soul!
> I mean to praise Yahweh all my life,
> I mean to sing to my God as long as I live. Alleluia!
> (Ps. 146:1–2)

+ As the time of your prayer draws to a conclusion, spend twenty minutes in quiet contemplative prayer.

+ Close your prayer with an Our Father.

+ Review of Prayer: Record in your journal the thoughts and feelings that have surfaced during your prayer.

Beside the Streams of Babylon

Complimentary prayer: The Phoenix (Part 1)

In this prayer period, use the introductory and closing framework of the previous prayer.

Prayerfully read the story of the Phoenix as told by Clement of Rome, AD 95. Allow yourself to imaginatively enter into the story.

> Let us look at the strange phenomenon that takes place in the East, that is, in the regions near Arabia. There is a bird that is called the Phoenix. This bird, the only one of its species, lives five hundred years. As the time of its dissolution in death approaches, it makes a nest of incense and myrrh and other spices, into which it enters when its time is completed, and dies. Now, as its flesh decays, a worm is born, which is nourished by the moisture of the dead bird, and grows wings. Then, growing strong, it picks up that nest, in which are the bones of its predecessor, and carries them from the country of Arabia as far as Egypt, to the city of Heliopolis. And in the daylight, in the sight of all, flying to the altar of the Sun, it places them there and so sets out on its return. Then the priests look up the records of the years, and they find that it has come at the end of the five hundredth year.
> (From "The Letter to the Corinthians,"" *The Apostolic Fathers*)

Consider:

> What images were the most vivid?
> What feelings surfaced within you?

Are there areas of your life in which you resonate with the Phoenix; for instance, experiences in which you have realized a sense of newness which has arisen following an experience of diminishment?

> Jesus says:

> The Father loves me,
> because I lay down my
> life in order to take it up
> again. No one takes it
> from me;
> I lay it down of my own free will
> and as it is in my power to lay it down
> so it is in my power to take it up again. (John 10:17–18)

Prayerfully read and reread these words of Jesus. Read them as if he is speaking directly to you. Open yourself to receive his words deep within your heart.

After spending some time absorbing Christ's words, enter into a conversation with him, first one speaking and then the other. Write this entire dialog.

Me_____
Jesus_____
Me_____

Allow this dialogue to proceed slowly and to flow naturally. Particularly, allow space for Jesus to speak.

You might consider sharing images or feelings that surfaced when you pondered Christ's words; you may choose to ask for guidance in your own "phoenix" experience.

Beside the Streams of Babylon

Complimentary prayer: The Phoenix Nest (Part2)

In this prayer period, use the introductory and closing framework of the previous prayer.

Reread the Phoenix story from the previous complimentary prayer.

The Phoenix built its nest of three precious and fragrant spices: frankincense, myrrh, and cassia. The phoenix constructed *his* own altar on which he "laid down" and "took up" his life.

In the spirit of Jesus who said, "I lay down my life in order to take it up again," imaginatively and consciously prepare and claim your "altar/nest."

Begin by drawing a large nest.

Consider the spices that make up your nest.

Frankincense

Frankincense was traditionally used in the offering of sacrifice, for the purpose of praising God and exorcising evil spirits.

Write in your nest/altar what in your life will comprise your "frankincense offering."

Myrrh

Myrrh is one of the principal spices used in ancient times; it was a symbol of suffering and purification.

> Write in your nest/altar how specific events have added the "fragrance of myrrh" to your life.

Cassia

Cassia was a spice used in the sanctuary for the purpose of anointing. It was believed to have a purgative, cleansing effect. In the Far East, it also signified immortality.

> Write in your nest/altar where in your life you experience a need for cleansing and clarification in order to come to a greater wholeness and holiness.

Spend some time in quiet stillness, allowing to deepen within yourself the awareness of the images, feelings, and insights that have surfaced during this time of prayer.

In the spirit of St. Ignatius, pray,

> Take, Lord, and receive all my liberty, my
> memory, my understanding and my entire will.
> All I have and call my own. You have given all to
> me. To you, Lord, I return it.

Everything is yours, do with it what you will.
Give me only your love and your grace,
That is enough for me.

The Tears of Jesus

Luke 19:41–42

> As Jesus drew near Jerusalem, he saw the city and wept over it, saying, "If this day you only knew what makes for peace—but now it is hidden from your eyes."

Commentary:

As Jesus came down the Mount of Olives, he was met with an incredible view of the spread of the beloved city of Jerusalem. The sun reflected on the magnificent structure of the temple that was the focus of the city. Jesus knows what is going on in the city. He is aware of the needless pain and suffering that is the result of political intrigue and power struggle. He knows that the refusal to follow the will of God is leading to a devastating destruction of the city and the temple. He is overwhelmed with grief.

Jesus weeps. He weeps because he loves his people and is filled with compassion for them. "The tears of Jesus are the tears of God…" (Johnson 1991, 241).

Like Jeremiah before him (13:17), and Nehemiah (1:4), Jesus weeps over the world he knew. It is not hard to think of Jesus—and our God—weeping, laboring, over our world today. How aware are we?

In a reflection on Luke 19:41–42, A. Alexander, SJ, draws on and includes the experience and words of Pope Francis, who calls us to enter into the tears of Jesus.

When Pope Francis went to the island of Lampedusa, where a boat of refuges had sunk and many had lost their lives, he asked if we have forgotten to grieve. He asked us if, in our world today, anyone feels "responsible" for what happened there.

He said:

> The culture of well-being, that makes us think of ourselves, that makes us live in soap bubbles, that are beautiful but are nothing, are illusions of futility, of the transient, that brings indifference to others, that brings even the globalization of indifference. We are accustomed to the suffering of others, it doesn't concern us, it is none of our business.
>
> We are a society that has forgotten the experience of weeping, of "suffering with" the globalization of indifference has taken from us the ability to weep.

What is it that will awaken in us the love and compassion that brings us to tears? In the garden of the resurrection, Jesus asked Mary, "Woman, why are you weeping?" (John 20:21). Evidently tears are not incompatible with the resurrection, but a part of the mission that sends us to bring the good news to our brothers and sisters. (John 21:17b–18)

Let us in the spirit of Jesus, and in company with Pope Francis, "ask the Lord for the grace to weep over our indifference, to weep over the cruelty in the world, in ourselves, and even in those who anonymously make socio-economic decisions that open the way to tragedies like this."

May our tears be the tears of God as we labor with and in him to bring peace to the world.

The Tears of Jesus

Suggested approach to prayer: A Prayer of Lamentation

+ Daily prayer plan (Orientations p. xxxi)

I quiet myself and relax in the presence of God.

I declare my dependency of God.

Grace: I beg for the grace of an intimate knowledge of the sharing of goods that God does in his love of me and in particular
how God labors and enters into the struggle of life. Filled with
gratitude, I want to be empowered just as totally in my love and
service of God.

Method: Meditation (Orientations p. xxxiv)

In the book of Lamentations, there is a description of the city of
Jerusalem, a city left empty and desolate in the time of exile.
Read it prayerfully. In what ways do you recognize much of our
culture in the description?

> Oh, how lonely she sits,
> the city once
> thronged with
> people, as if
> suddenly widowed.
> Though once great among the nations,
> she, the princess among the provinces

is now reduced to vassalage.
She passes her nights weeping; the tears run down her cheeks.
(Lam. 1:1–2)

Where in your family, community, country, world, are you most aware of the suffering and oppression of people?

+ Allow yourself to enter into the pain of these people. Bring your tears into concrete prayers.

+ Ask for an awareness of your own share in creating the conditions that foster this oppression.

+ How will your tears move you to action?

Make your own the prayer of Pope Francis:

O Lord, we ask forgiveness for the indifference toward so many brothers and sisters. We ask forgiveness for those who are pleased with themselves, who are closed in on their own well-being in a way that leads to the anesthesia of the heart. We ask you, Father, for forgiveness for those who with their decisions at the global level have created situations that lead to these tragedies.

Forgive us, lord.

+ As the time of your prayer draws to a conclusion, spend twenty minutes in quiet contemplative prayer.

+ Close your prayer with an Our Father.

+ Review of Prayer: Record in your journal the thoughts and feelings that have surfaced during your prayer.

The Tears of Jesus

Complimentary prayer/exercise: Sufferings in the World

In this prayer period, use the introductory and closing framework of the previous prayer in the creation of the suggested collage.

Using the passage Luke 19:41–42, make a collage of pictures of suffering in our world today. Keep it before you, in your office, or on your prayer table.

Let it be the backdrop of your work and your prayer.

The Cross of Love

John 19:28–34

After this, Jesus knew that everything had now been completed, and to fulfill the scripture perfectly he said: "I am thirsty." A jar full of vinegar stood there, so putting a sponge soaked in the vinegar on a hyssop stick they held it up to his mouth. After Jesus had taken the vinegar he said, "It is accomplished"; bowing his head, he gave up his spirit.

It was the Preparation Day, and to prevent the bodies remaining on the cross during the Sabbath...the Jews asked Pilate to have the leg broken and the bodies taken away.

Consequently the soldiers came and broke the legs of the first man who had been crucified with him and then of the other. When they came to Jesus, they found he was already dead, and so instead of breaking his legs one of the soldiers pierced his side with a lance; and immediately there came out blood and water.

Commentary:

If you have been fortunate enough to have witnessed a mother giving birth, you will recall how the agony of her birth contractions quickly gave way to the exuberant joy of the baby birthed. In her suffering we *see* love!

"A woman in childbirth suffers, because her time has come; but when she has given birth to the child, she forgets the suffering in her joy that a child has been born into the world." (John 16:21)

When a mother and father describe the birth of their new baby, they rarely speak of the pain of the birth process. On the contrary, in the joy of the mother and father, we witness their willingness to embrace the suffering that is always the consequence of creative love.

When we see the cross, we see the labor of love!

The suffering of Christ on the cross is real. He is enduring the excruciating pain of birthing the spirit into the world. It is love that has brought him to this point, a love that is passionate, extravagant, and wasteful as only God's love can be.

While the blood and water that flow out of his wounded side can be explained medically, John sees this as a sign. With the death of Christ and the release of the Spirit, the life-giving work of the Church begins. In a sense one can say that from the wounded side of Christ, the Church is born.

We have failed to see the wisdom of the cross when we have assimilated and fostered, in a distorted way, an emphasis of sin over love as if, the primary meaning of the death of Jesus is a punishment willed by the father to make up for and save us from our sins. While it is true, that the death does, indeed, save us from our sinfulness, it is not from the perspective of punishment but rather from God's overwhelming faithfulness and tender loving kindness for us. St. Bonaventure says, "God's love is so abundant that God is willing to plunge into the darkness of humanity to bring us into the fullness of life…God could not bend over any further in love for us than in the suffering and death of the cross" (Delio 2005, 52–53).

In John's Gospel, Jesus goes willingly to his death. He has lived his life challenging the sinful structures of his culture. His activities were seen as subversive to the present regime and, not surprisingly, led to his execution. He knew his destiny; he knew his time had come and he chose it. He consciously chose to live his life out of his deepest conviction of his Father's love, whatever the cost.

The image of Jesus's body [crucified on the cross] is a standing icon of what humanity is doing and what God suffers "with," "in," and "through" us. It is an icon of utter divine solidarity with our pain and our problems…It is our central transformative image for the soul. Whenever you see an image of the crucified Jesus, know that it is the clear and central message unveiled. It reveals what humanity is doing to itself and to one another. Don't lessen its meaning by making it merely into a mechanical transaction whereby Jesus pays some "price" to God or the devil. The only price paid is to the intransigent human soul—so it can see! (Rohr 2011, 137–38).

To embrace Christ is to identify with and to embrace the cross, to consciously labor with God. St. Ignatius is an example of the call to each baptized person. On his way to Rome, he and his companions stopped at a chapel at La Storta. While there, Ignatius had what can only be called a peak experience. He had a vision of Jesus carrying his cross, and he heard the Father say to Jesus, "I want this man to serve us." Ignatius experienced his vocation as a call to be "placed with the Son." In his mission and in the death and resurrection. The cross would lead him to enter into the pain of the world and to labor there with and through Christ.

> His cross stretched from the inner heart of God to the depths of human darkness. As the cross plunges into the roots of Creation's darkness it enters the pain of war, hatred, fear, resistance, violence, abuse, injury, rape,
>
> vengeance, terrorism, the cross of every violation of the human spirit that seeks to destroy the goodness of the human person and nature itself. Because the cross begins in the heart of God's overflowing love it brings with it the power of love into the places where humans have failed to image God. (Delio 2005, 154–55)

Jesus accepted death as the completion of God's plan for him. The words "it is accomplished" are in essence a victory cry. With his death his spirit is released. The incredible energy of his love, freed from the constraints of his human body, expands and extends to all people for all time. His spirit of love permeates all of creation, the entire universe. That same spirit empowers us to lay down our lives, as did Ignatius, in emulation of him. We, too, are enabled to bring God's love into the depths of human darkness.

Within the circumstances of our own lives, we labor with and in the Spirit of God to bring new life and joy into the world.

It begins with love; it ends with love! "Suffering does not have the last word"! (Delio 2005, 141).

The Cross of Love

Suggested approach to prayer: At the Cross

+ Daily prayer plan   (Orientations p.xxxi)

   I quiet myself and relax in the presence of God.

   I declare my dependency on God.

Grace: I beg for the gift of an intimate knowledge of goods that God does in his love for me, and in particular how God labors and enters into the struggle of life. Filled with gratitude, I want to be empowered just as totally in my love and service of God.

Method: Meditation   (Orientations p.xxxiv)

I sit before the cross of Christ. For several minutes, I gaze, as into a mirror, on the image of Christ crucified.

As you gaze on the cross, what questions are reflected?

+ Why did Jesus do this? What is the meaning of this? What is the Love that would prompt so great a willingness to suffer and lay down one's life?

+ What does the cross reveal to me about who God is and how God continues to labor for me?

+ What implications does the cross have for me?

+ How am I being called, within the circumstances and events of my life, to descend into the suffering and pain, the darkness, which I see and experience?

+ What new life do I experience being birthed within the struggles and sufferings of my life and among those I encounter?

+ Can I be courageous enough to live in the joy of God's love while, at the same time, I am aware that the darkness is deep within our culture, individually and collectively?

In confidence, make your own the following prayer:

> Jesus, may all that is you flow into me.
> May your body and blood be my food and drink.
> May your passion and death be my strength and life.
> Jesus, with you by my side enough has been given.
>
> May the shelter I seek be the shadow of your cross.
> Let me not run from the love which you offer,
> But hold me safe from the forces of evil.
> On each of my dyings shed your light and your love.
> Keep calling to me until that day comes,
> When, with your saints, I may praise you forever. Amen.
> ("Soul of Christ," paraphrased by D. L. Fleming, SJ)

+ As the time of your prayer draws to a conclusion, spend twenty minutes in quiet contemplative prayer.

+ Close your prayer with an Our Father.

+ Review of Prayer: Record in your journal the thoughts and feelings that have surfaced during your prayer.

The Passion Today

Matthew 10:39

> ...whoever loses his/her life for my sake will find it.

Commentary:

Where is the Passion of Christ most alive in today's world?

The passion of Christ is most alive in our world today in those people who, in the spirit of Jesus, have embraced the reality of their own death and having entered into the mystery of it, consequently spend their lives, with courage and freedom, in self-forgetful, compassionate service.

John English, SJ, wrote that it is happening in the lives of those who have "moved beyond themselves toward Christ in much the same way Jesus moved out of himself through the Passion. Jesus gives himself for others; he forgets himself. He is concerned about the disciples.

> He reaches out to Pilate...He comforts the women... pardons the good thief, provides for the care of Mary..." (English 1995, 218–19).

Today, in the midst of much brokenness, there is pain everywhere. People are traumatized by the insecurity and threat of terrorism. We live in a time when we are less and less able to live in isolation from the pain and brokenness that are part and parcel of our human existence. We no longer have the luxury of withdrawing to the middle-class and perhaps upper-class comfort and security into which we are so easily co-opted.

We look for and we find the witness of people in whom the passion of Christ is most alive.

We are humbled before the lives of service and the deaths of people like Dorothy Stang, Archbishop Romero, and Gandhi. We are touched by those in our families and neighborhood who pour out their lives for a handicapped child, or a spouse with Alzheimer.

One woman's story allows us entry into the mystery of the passage from death into life.

On May 12, 2008, a ninety-eight-year-old woman, Irena Sendler, died in her apartment in Warsaw, Poland. Remembering her story is an experience of the living out of the Passion in today's world. When Irena was seven, she lost her father, a physician, to typhus that he contracted as he treated the poor. When he was dying, he told his little daughter, "If you see someone drowning you must try to rescue them, even if you cannot swim."

In 1939, the Nazis swept through Poland and imprisoned the Jews in ghettos where they were first starved to death and then systematically murdered in killing camps. Irena, by then a social worker in Warsaw, saw the Jewish people "drowning" and resolved to do what she could to rescue as many as possible, especially the children. Working with a network of other social workers and brave Poles, mostly women, she smuggled twenty-five hundred children out of the Warsaw ghetto and hid them safely until the end of the war.

Irena took great risks—obtaining forged papers for the children, disguising herself as an infection control nurse, diverting German occupation funds for the support of children in hiding. She entered the ghetto, sometimes two or three times a day, and talked Jewish parents into giving up their children. Irena drugged the babies with sedatives and smuggled them past Nazi guards in gunnysacks, boxers, and coffins. She helped the older ones escape through the sewers, through secret opening in the wall, through the courthouse, through churches, any clever way she and her network could evade the Nazis.

Once outside the ghetto walls, Sendler gave the children false names and documents and placed them with Polish families, in convents and orphanages. With the hope that after the war she could reunite the children with surviving relatives, she kept thin tissue paper lists of each child's Jewish name, Polish name, and address, and hid the precious lists in glass jars buried under an apple tree in the back yard of one of her coconspirators.

In 1943, Irena was arrested, tortured—both legs and feet were broken—and sentenced to death by a firing squad. She never divulged the location of her Polish underground contacts. At the last moment, she was saved by the Polish underground association that bribed a guard to secure her freedom. Until recently her story and that of the other courageous Poles with whom she worked was buried and forgotten.

Irena spent the last years of her life, living in a small apartment with relatives, able to walk only with crutches, still grieving the children she was not able to save.

Surely, there was a moment in her life, when Irena, like Jesus, was faced with the meaning of her life, and in that moment crossed over into freedom; at that moment she embraced her destiny. It was her Gethsemane moment. Was it the time of her father's death…or the night before she went into the ghetto for the first time?

Where is the Passion of Christ alive today? In the hearts, in the passion for life in men and women like Irena Sendler, and Romero, and Stang, and the firemen who risked their lives in rescuing people on 9/11. Each was called to face, as each of us is called to face, a Gethsemane moment, a Passover moment. "To lose one's life, therefore refers not only to martyrdom but in given circumstances to the surrender of one's secure bourgeois existence for the sake of the reign of God" (Lohfink 2012, 218).

The Passion of Christ is most alive in our world today in those people who, in the Spirit of Jesus, have embraced the reality of their death, and having entered into the mystery of it, have passed form death to a life spent in self—forgetful, compassionate service, and do so in freedom and with courage and even with joy. They know in their hearts the promise of Jesus, that those who lose their lives for his sake find life.

The Passion Today

Suggested approach to prayer: Take Up Your Cross

+ Daily prayer plan   (Orientations p. xxxi)

I quiet myself and relax in the presence of God.

I declare my dependency on God.

+ Grace: I beg for the gift of an intimate knowledge of the sharing of goods that God does in his love for me, and in particular how God labors and enters into the struggles of life. Filled with gratitude, I want to be empowered to respond just as totally in my love and service of God.

Method: Meditative Reading   (Orientations p. xxxviii)

I ponder the words of Jesus, inviting us to "take up your cross and follow me" (Mark 8:34). Prayerfully, and meditatively, reread Irena Sendler's story.

> Where do you find yourself pausing to absorb the courage and willingness to embrace the pain of those she is trying to serve?
>
> What do you want to say to her?
>
> How do you think she might respond to you?

What are the situations, the people in your life, that are occasions for embracing and laboring, in the spirit of Jesus, to relieve their pain and suffering?

Reflect on the following counsel:

When burdened with great crosses, do not let your heart yearn for death. Let it be enough for you to be crucified with Jesus Christ, as much as and in a way that is pleasing to God, and regarding every circumstance of your life and death, let God decide. (Medaille 1979)

Ask, again, for the grace you most need.

+ As the time of prayer draws to a conclusion, spend twenty minutes in quiet contemplative prayer.

+ Conclude with an Our Father.

+ Review of Prayer: Record in your journal the thoughts and feelings that have surfaced during your prayer.

Passion Today

Complimentary prayer: Gethsemane Moment

In this prayer period, use the introductory and closing framework of the previous prayer.

Method, Lectio Divina (Orientations p. xxxvi)

Lectio: Gently and prayerfully read and reread the words of the Gospel: "Whoever losses his/her life for my sake will find it..."

Meditatio: Who are the people in your life in whom you see the Passion of Christ being lived out?

There are Gethsemane moments in the lives of each of us, that is, when we are faced with the meaning of life and are given a choice whether or not to embrace the reality of our deaths, and to really surrender and to enter into and embrace the pain of others.

What has been your Gethsemane moment?

How is the Passion of Christ alive in you?

Oratio: Ask for the grace to deeply embrace your life and death in the Spirit of Jesus, and to "let go" in compassionate service to those who suffer.

Contemplatio: Spend twenty minutes or so in contemplative prayer.

The Passion Today

Complimentary prayer: Will You Wake?

In this prayer period, use the introductory and closing framework of the previous prayer.

Method: Poetry as Prayer (Orientations p. xxxix)

The human heart can go to the lengths of God.
Dark and cold we may be, this
is no winter now. The frozen misery
of centuries breaks, cracks, begins to move,
the thunder is the thunder of the floes,
the thaw, the flood, the upstart spring.
Thank God our time is now when wrong
comes up to face us everywhere,
never to leave us till we take
the longest stride of soul men and women ever took.
Affairs are now soul size.
The enterprise
is exploration into God.
Where are you making for?
It takes so many thousand years to wake,
but will you wake for pity's sake?
                    ("A Sleep of Prisoners," C. Fry)

Repetition Day: God labors in and for me.

Grace: I beg for the gift of an intimate knowledge of the sharing of goods that God does in his love for me, and in particular how God labors and for me. Filled with gratitude, I want to be empowered to respond just as totally in my love and service of God.

Approach to prayer: Repetition   (Orientations p.xlii)

In preparation, I review my prayer by rereading my journal of the past days. I select for my repetition the period of prayer that most reveals to me the awareness of how God is always laboring, entering into the very struggle of life, and in which I was deeply moved by joy, amazement, gratitude, or awe. I proceed in the manner I did originally, focusing on the scene, word, feeling, or passage that was previously most significant. I may choose to return to a passage with which I had difficulty.

I consider how, like any reasonable person, I am moved to respond to this God who labors for me, to bring forth new life. Moved by love, I may find that I can best respond in the words of the following prayer of St. Ignatius:

> Take, Lord, and receive all my liberty, my memory, my understanding, and my entire will—all that I have and call my own. You have given it all to me. To you, Lord, I return it. Everything is yours; do with it what you will. Give me only your love and your grace. That is enough for me.

Review of prayer: I write in my journal any feelings, experiences, or insights that have come to my awareness with a particular significance during this prayer period.

Point 5

God as Giver and Gift

God's love shines down upon me like the light rays from the sun, or his love is poured forth lavishly like a fountain spilling forth its waters into an unending stream. Just as I see the sun in its rays and the fountain in its waters, so God pours forth himself in all the gifts that he showers upon me. God cannot do enough to speak out his love for me always calling me to a fuller and better life.

Spiritual Exercises, #237

GIFT FROM ABOVE

James 1:16–18

> Make no mistake about this, my dear sisters and brothers: it is all that is good, everything that is perfect, which is given us from above; it comes down from the Father of all light; with him there is no such thing as alteration, no shadow of a change. By his own choice he made us his children by the message of the truth so that we should be a sort of first fruits of all that he had created.

Commentary:

"Every morning God says to the sun 'get up and shine'" (Attributed to G. K. Chesterton).

For eons, the sun has "been radiating her life energy toward Earth, ceaselessly pouring four million tons of herself every second…just like the sunlight, God's grace has always been radiating toward Earth, ceaselessly self-communicating, ceaselessly pushing for life from within and without" (Cannoto 2006, 74).

While the rays of the sun are received by the earth in seasonal fluctuation as the earth revolves around the sun, the gift of God's light and grace are constant, perfect, and unchanging. Just as our very existence is totally dependent on the outpouring energy of the sun, so, too, without the gift of God's love and grace, we would become as barren and desolate as the earth deprived of the sun.

But, "make no mistake about this" God's love is creative, all embracing. We are held tenderly as God's beloved and precious children within the rays of this love.

Lord my God, when your love spilled over into creation
You thought of me.
I am
from love of love for love.
(Bergan and Schwan 1985, 11)

Because God has "loved us first" (1 John 4, 19) and filled us with his light, we experience God's love in our very being and in all that we encounter. As a result of this experience, we become aware of our great need of God. Ignatius of Loyola speaks of this experience as that of creaturehood. In the Spiritual Exercises, he emphasizes God as loving Creator and we as creatures. To the degree that our hearts are open to God's love and light of grace we are led to the awareness that everything is gift. Our response is praise, reverence, and service.

This consciousness of dependency on God expresses itself as a joyful poverty. Johannes B. Metz in his classic *Poverty of Spirit* details and clarifies the concrete shapes that this poverty can assume.

The following is drawn from his book.

There is the *poverty of commonplace* in which the individual experiences his- or herself as being part of the common lot, ordinary, no one special. We see in Jesus this poverty of commonplace: he was a simple man; "he had no talent but that of his own heart, no contribution to make except self-abandonment, no consolation save God alone."

There is the *poverty of misery and neediness* in which the primary expression is having nothing of one's own to provide security except hope and trust. Jesus knew hunger, exile, and the loneliness of the outcast. In Jesus's willingness to enter into this form of poverty, he showed how even this neediness can become blessed.

There is also the *poverty of uniqueness and superiority* in which exceptional gifts and talents set one apart and often lead to a sense of being burdened and lonely. In the temptation in the desert, we see the Evil One tempting Jesus to renounce his unique mission.

Closely related to the poverty of uniqueness is the *poverty of our provisional and transient nature as human beings.* It is the experience of the prophet when everything within strains forward and is set on edge in anticipation. The individual experiences everything as incomplete and wanting.

The *poverty of encounter* occurs whenever we are called on to forget ourselves in order to be open to the other. Every stirring of genuine love makes us poor. For the true lover must be vulnerable and unprotected and give him- or herself without reservation or question.

Finally, there is the *poverty of diminishment and death* in which a person slips away from himself or herself entirely. All the other forms of poverty are the prelude and the testing ground for the critical moment of death.

Metz's work does us a great service. The awareness of the various forms that the poverty of our creaturehood can assume allows one to identify and embrace the human condition within oneself and therein to seek the unique gift and grace of God's goodness and presence revealed within the specific poverty one experiences.

Seeing the Creator's faithfulness of loving presence leads one to choose, to elect, and to entrust oneself in total abandonment to God. In this new consciousness, all falls away and one can be content with either health or sickness, wealth or poverty, honor or dishonor, long life or short life. In this new-found freedom, our hearts joyfully sing,

"May I never seek nor choose to be other than You intend or wish."

(Bergan and Schwan 1985, 11)

Gift from Above

Suggested approach to prayer: Hidden Blessings

+ Daily prayer plan   (Orientations p. xxxi)

 I quiet myself and relax in the presence of God.

 I declare my dependency on God.

Grace: I beg for the gift of an intimate knowledge of the sharing of goods that God does in his love for me and how, at every moment and in every way, the many gifts of God's love inundate and surround me. Filled with gratitude, I want to be empowered to respond just as totally in my love and service of God.

Method: Meditation   (Orientations p.xxxiv)

Prayerfully reread the passage from James. Let the words be heard in the depths of your inner self.

+ Reflecting on the various forms of poverty described in the commentary, identify the one that most expresses your experience.

 How does your form of poverty show itself?

 In which ways do you resist or resent this configuration within you?

 To what extent have you been able to acknowledge, own, and embrace your poverty?

As you reflect on your life, the circumstances, and events, what have been the grace and gifts of your particular poverty? How has your poverty blessed you?

How does your poverty prompt you toward dependency on God? Where would you have been without your particular poverty?

+ Write a prayer declaring your dependency on God and of thanksgiving and praise for the gifts that have flowed from your particular poverty.

+ As the time of my prayer draws to a conclusion, spend twenty minutes in quiet contemplative prayer.

+ Close your prayer with an Our Father.

+ Review of Prayer: Record in your journal the thoughts and feelings that have surfaced during your prayer.

Living in the Divine Milieu

Romans 8:35, 38–39

> Nothing therefore can come between us and the love of Christ, even if we are troubled or worried, or being persecuted, or lacking food or clothes, or being threatened or even attacked…For I am certain of this: neither death nor life, no angel, no prince, nothing that exists, nothing still to come, not any power, or height or depth, nor any creative thing, can ever come between us and the love of God made visible in Christ Jesus our Lord.

Commentary:

How encouraging! We will never be alone! There simply is nothing that will keep us from God—nothing!

Not only will we not be separated from the love of God in Christ but the very things that we are most fearful of will themselves reveal the presence of God. May we have eyes to see them as gifts. For those who love God, life in all its pain and joy is transparent of God's love.

The secret is in the believing. "If we believe, everything is illuminated and takes shape around us, risk no longer exists, and success takes on an incorruptible fullness; pain becomes a visit and a caress from God…"

"Oh ye of little faith, why have you doubted me?"
(Dupleix 1999,6)

In commenting on this passage from Romans, Teilhard de Chardin says, that while agreeing with St. Paul's thinking that love is a force greater than all other forces, he expands this idea, perceiving God's love as a *dynamic* and penetrating energy which embraces and super-animates all things. Teilhard names this energizing phenomenon the "*divine milieu...*" (Faricy 1981, 26–27).

Choosing to consciously live in this divine milieu is to nurture within oneself a familiarity with God that leads to an experience of oneness with God, an intimacy that the mystics name as union. Embraced within this grace of intimacy and mystical awareness of God, everything becomes an occasion of an encounter with God and expresses and radiates the limitlessness of God's love.

If only we knew how to look at life as God sees it, we would perceive that nothing in the world is profane, but that everything contributes to the building of the Kingdom of God. To have faith is not only to raise one's eyes to God to contemplate him; it is also to look at this world—but with Christ's eyes. If we had allowed Christ to penetrate our whole being, if we had sufficiently made our gaze single, the world would no longer be an obstacle. It would be a perpetual incentive to work for the Father in order that, in Christ, his Kingdom might come on earth as it is in heaven (M. Quoist, quoted Cusson 1989, 139–140).

As we consciously choose to cultivate an experience of "seeing God in all things," it follows that we will be called to develop within ourselves a disciplined practice of fostering our cooperation with God's grace. The forms and possibilities of this practice are myriad and the particular spiritual practices need to be chosen and developed with a gentle awareness of one's individual personality and disposition.

Primarily, one's spiritual practice must include a commitment to personal, regular solitary prayer that has as its focus the word of God as found in scripture. The scriptures may be approached through the use of Ignatian contemplation or meditation on God's word as a love letter, or the process of *Lectio Divina*. An essential enhancement of the praying of scripture is the practice of centering prayer that serves as the pathway to contemplative prayer. Supportive to a life that desires to emulate and follow the path of Christ is Ignatius's daily Examen in which one can discern how faithfully one has been aware of God's presence and how one has responded to God's love. Complementary to our life of prayer is the practice of spiritual reading where we glean the wisdom of our spiritual ancestors and current spiritual authors. Spiritual direction can prove to be an invaluable asset in the development of our spiritual life (Cf. Orientations).

Innate within our human spirit is the great need and desire to share our life in God with others. This desire is met in worship as we communally participate in the sacramental life of our Church. From the moment we are born to the moment we die, we are in blessed relationship, simultaneously, with God and each other: we are birthed anew in Baptism, nourished at the table of

Eucharist, confirmed and sealed with the Holy Spirit, joined together in love through Christian marriage, consecrated to service
through Holy Orders and religious vows, and finally forgiven,
healed, and ushered into life eternal. Integral to our sacramental life is the official prayer of the Church, the precious tradition
known as the Divine Office that blesses us with an experience
of solidarity with others. How magnificent is it to realize that the
prayer of the Office, like Eucharist, is at every moment being offered somewhere on our planet.

All these treasures of grace speak to us of God's magnanimous
generosity!

The spiritual practices that we embrace provide a framework,
structure, and support for a way of life, a manner of living that
the early followers of St. Ignatius spoke of as being *contemplative in action.* These practices nurture our relationship with God
so that we are graced to be attentive to and to consciously recognize God's activity within our lives. The words and actions that
flow in response to the circumstances and events we experience
become, themselves, graced with God's presence. In our faithfulness to being attentive to God's presence, that is, keeping our
gaze focused on God, our lives, themselves, become a revelation, an icon of God's presence. This is all God's work! God is
actively laboring to form Christ within us and thereby to bring
about the Kingdom.

Living in the Divine Milieu

Suggested Approach to Prayer: Growing in Awareness

+ Daily prayer plan   (Orientations p. xxxi)

I quiet myself and relax in the presence of God. I declare my dependency on God.

Whether or not one has a firmly established spiritual practice, it is invaluable periodically to reflect on the practices to which one has committed himself or herself. In this prayer period, following the form of the Ignatian Examen of Consciousness, prayerfully consider your life of prayer during the past year. Include not only the formal times of prayer but how that prayer has had implications for your daily life.

Reflect on the challenging counsel of Father Medaille as he invites us to undivided surrender to the gift of God:

Be utterly given to God by a holy self-surrender, utterly for God by a love pure and completely unselfish, utterly in God by a continuing effort to be more conscious of God's presence, utterly according to God by a will, a life and everything conformed to God.

Method: Examen of Consciousness   (Orientations p. xliii)

God, our Creator, I am totally dependent on you. All is gift. I give you thanks and praise for the many gifts of prayer I have received during the past year.

+ As you contemplate the past year of your life, identify the gifts that arose from your prayer, both solitary and communal. For instance, did you experience peace, guidance, inspiration, and so on.

Lord, I believe you work through and in time to reveal me to myself. Please give me an increased awareness of how you are guiding and shaping my life, as well as a more sensitive awareness of the obstacles I put in your way.

You have been present in my life this past year. Be near, now, as I reflect on my spiritual practices:

+ Referring to the commentary, list the practices to which you have committed. Reflect how, in each of them, God's presence and love has shown itself.

+ Reflect on the feelings and insights that accompanied your experiences.

+ Within the context of the commentary, reflect on how you have experienced your prayer practices gracing your daily life.

+ How, in your present commitment of spiritual practices, do you experience God calling you to assess and adapt your prayer practices to better mirror where you are in your life at this time.

+ Reflect on how, in this past year, you have responded to your inner urges and yearning for a more intimate relationship with God?

Gracious God, I ask your loving forgiveness and healing.

+ As I reflect on my spiritual practices during the past year, for what am I most regretful and for what am I most in need of forgiveness and healing?

Filled with hope and a firm belief, I entrust myself to your care and commit myself to the following practices of prayer.

You may consider this commitment as your personal "rule of life" (Orientations xlix).

+ As the time of your prayer draws to a conclusion, spend twenty minutes in quiet contemplative prayer.

+ Close your prayer with an Our Father.

+ Review of Prayer: Record in your journal the thoughts and feelings that have surfaced during your prayer.

Explosion of Love

John 20:19–21

> In the evening of that same day, the first day of the week, the doors were closed in the room where the disciples were, for fear of the Jews. Jesus came and stood among them. He said to them, "Peace be with you," and showed them his hands and his side. The disciples were filled with joy when they saw the Lord, and he said to them again, "Peace be with you. As the Father sent me, so I am sending you."

Commentary:

He was gone. They would never hear the sound of his voice again. He would never again speak their names. He was gone where they could not follow.

Suddenly, he is present! The one they loved, Jesus, is with them. They see him. He speaks to them. He is the same, yet he is different.

> Christianity is based on several core beliefs that are shocking. One is that God becomes a human person, a carpenter turned preacher. The other *is* that a dead man is raised to new life. (Delio 2011, 72)

Peanuts has something to say! In a popular cartoon, a thirsty Snoopy carries his empty water bowl between his teeth. We see him standing under the backyard faucet. He is trying to figure out how, at the same time, he can turn on the faucet while holding the bowl in his teeth. Suddenly, the heavens open, and a huge cloudburst fills his bowl to the brim. As Snoopy walks away, the bubble over his head says, "I'm going to have to think about this one for a long time."

We, as followers of Jesus, even believing as we do in the Resurrection, need to seriously think about the Resurrection. We need not only to have a grasp of the official theological teaching about it but it is critical that we prayerfully ponder the implication of the resurrection in our personal lives.

We owe a great debt of gratitude to scripture scholars and theologians who have consistently enriched our understanding of the sacred text that describe the early Christian experience of the Resurrection. It is not, however, an easy task to comprehend and assimilate the plethora of insights that results from their dedicated research and study. This is especially true when interpretations are diverse and multilayered. Complexity can outstrip one's ability to grasp and integrate the new teachings into the core reality scripture intends. Even more disconcerting is that some of the new· theology may seem to be contrary to the tradition we have always embraced. But still, even though we may feel at times threatened, we must be open and discerning in our trusting of the unfolding revelation of the Spirit in the hearts and voices of those of our time. It is not at all easy. Some of the teachings may seem so radical as to deny the central truth of the Resurrection, that is, having died, the body of Christ rose from the dead.

Finally, we cannot allow our fear to serve as an obstacle to a greater enhancement of the central mystery of the Resurrection and its implications for the heart of our spirituality and lives. "Every age must discover Christ anew" (Delio 2008, 40).

In his April 15, 2006, Easter Vigil homily, Pope Benedict XVI describes the resurrection of Jesus:

The Resurrection is like an explosion of light, an explosion of love that dissolved the hitherto indissoluble compenetration of "dying and becoming." It ushered in a new dimension of being, a new dimension of life in which, in a transformed way, matter too was integrated and through which a new world emerges. It is clear that this event is not just some miracle from the past, the occurrence of which could be ultimately a matter of indifference to us. It is a qualitative leap in a history of "evolution" and of life in general toward a new future life, toward a new world that, starting from Christ, already continuously permeates this world of ours, transforms it and draws it to itself.

The Resurrection of Christ is an open door through which passes the pulsating and transforming energy of God empowering and animating all of creation, into a new way of being. The strength of this explosion of love and light launches a new world, propelling evolution forward.

> The world of the past has gone...Now I am making the whole of creation new...(Rev. 21:4b, 5)

Hope and beauty are unleashed!

Believing, we enter into freedom. The door of the resurrection opens us, with a dynamic new consciousness, to a changed way of thinking of ourselves. Our union and solidarity with Jesus, in his Paschal Mystery, is affirmed, giving us a clearer sense of our responsibility for and participation in his mission. Here and now in us and through us the resurrection continues. Here and now we are given the power of confidence and courage to live out of our true selves in God, and thereby, to shape this new world in peace and joy. In the Risen Christ, we experience God as giver and gift.

"What we are waiting for God to accomplish in the future is already a part of our lives right here and now." (Karban 2012, 2)

Explosion of Love

Suggested approach to prayer: Through Closed Doors

+ Daily prayer plan   (Orientations p. xxxi)

I quiet myself and relax in the presence of God.

I declare my dependency on God.

Grace: I beg for the gift of an intimate knowledge of the sharing of goods that God does in his love for me and how, at every moment and in every way, the many gifts of God's inundate and surround me. Filled with gratitude, I desire to be empowered to respond just as totally in my love and service of God.

Method: Ignatian Contemplation   (Orientations p. xxxiv)

+ Reread the Gospel passage. Using your imagination and employing all your senses enter into this Resurrection appearance of Jesus to his disciples.

See yourself with the disciples huddled together in fear behind locked doors, grieving the loss of Jesus.

Imagine that Jesus suddenly is there.

Be aware of your reaction. Fear? Shock? Gladness? Listen as he says to you, "Peace."

How does your heart respond?

What stirs within you as you hear him say, "As the Father has sent me, I am sending you."

+ Within the context of the Gospel and the commentary, how has belief in the resurrection:

—Influenced your sense of identity?

—Endowed you with a sense of freedom and clarity?

—Enabled you to make decisions with confidence?

—Strengthened your commitment to your vocation and service? Do you feel a greater sense of responsibility?

—Expanded your compassion and love toward others?

+ How is your belief in the Resurrection a gift?

Make your own the following prayer of Teilhard de Chardin, SJ

Glorious Lord Christ:
the divine influence secretly diffused and
active in the depths of matter,
and the dazzling center
where all the innumerable fibers of the manifold
meet; power as implacable as the world and as

warm as life; you whose forehead is of the
whiteness of snow, whose eyes are of fire,
and whose feet are brighter than molten gold;
you whose hands imprison the stars;
you who are the first and the last,
the living and the dead and the risen again;
you who gather into the exuberant
unity every mode of existence;
it is you to whom my being cries
out with a desire as vast as the
universe:
"In truth you are my Lord and my God." (Harter 1993/2005,
80)

+ As the time of your prayer draws to a conclusion, spend twenty
minutes in quiet contemplative prayer.

+ Close your prayer with an Our Father.

+ Review of Prayer: Record in your journal the thoughts and feelings that have surfaced during your prayer.

The Breath of the Spirit

John 20:21–23

> "As the Father has sent me, so I send you." And when
> he had said this, he breathed on them and said to them,
> "Receive the Holy Spirit. Whose sins you forgive are
> forgiven them, and whose sins you retain are retained."

Commentary:

"Blow on the coal of the heart, my dear. Blow on the coal of the
heart, and we'll see by and by."

These are the words of the wife of J. B. in the last scene of
Archibald MacLeish's drama *J. B.*, a contemporary interpretation
of the story of Job. In the last scene, the stage is stripped, and
after having lost his business, his home, his wife, his family, and in
a world ravaged by a nuclear devastation, J. B. sits center stage,
naked and depressed.

It is then that his wife walks on stage from the wings, carrying a
branch of golden spring flowers. "Look, Job"—calling him by
this name for the only time in the play—"Look, the forsythia...I
found it growing in the ashes, blooming in all that mountain of
broken glass." And then, tenderly, she says, "Blow on the coal of
the heart, my dear, and we'll see by and by. Blow on the coal of
the heart." (MacLeish 2006, scene 11, 626).

On the first Easter evening, the disciples are devastated, gathered in fear behind locked doors. All they had hoped for, dreamed

of, invested their time and energy into is lost. The One in whom they had placed their hopes is dead, buried. They sit in grief.

Then, suddenly, like a breath of spring, Jesus is with them. For all their failures, their lack of understanding through the three years of his teaching, for all their sense of loss, the Risen Christ sees within them a spark, like a smoldering in the ashes, in the hearts of these men whom he has so loved.

Wordlessly he looks deep into the eyes of each one and blows a gentle breath. Jesus breathes a breath, like the breath that gave life to Adam, and awakens them to the presence of his own Holy Spirit. It is a spirit of forgiveness for their own failures, a gift they will "by and by" bring to the world into which they are being sent.

In commenting on this passage, Richard Rohr says,

> We are all allowed to ride life and love's wonderful mystery for a few years—until life and love reveal themselves as the same thing, which is the final and full message of the risen Christ—life morphing into a love that is beyond space and time. He literally "breathes" shalom and forgiveness into the universal air. You get to add your own finishing touches of love, your own life breath to the Great Breath, and then return the completed package to its maker in a brand new but also same form. (Rohr 2013, 177–78)

The Breath of the Spirit

Suggest approach to prayer: The Coal of the Heart

+ Daily prayer plan (Orientations p. xxxi)

I quiet myself and relax in the presence of God. I declare my dependency on God.

Grace: I beg for the gift of an intimate knowledge of a sharing of goods that God does in his love for me and how, at every moment and in every way, the many gifts of God inundate and surround me. Filled with gratitude, I desire to be empowered to respond just as totally in my love and service of God.

Method: Ignatian Contemplation   (Orientations.p.xxxiv)

+ Read and reread the scripture passage, John 20:21–23.

See yourself as one of the disciples in the Upper Room, and open your heart to receive the breath of Jesus Risen.

Image your heart like a coal, still, but barely alight, in the ashes of your own experiences. Ponder: Where is your heart cold, perhaps ashen, yearning to catch fire?

Where in your heart is there a flickering of desire?

Unite your breath to that of Jesus's as he gently blows on your heart, awakening the dormant flame into life.

+ Prayerfully reread the passage.

+ As the time of prayer draws to a conclusion, spend twenty minutes in quiet contemplative prayer.

+ Close your prayer with an Our Father.

+ Review of Prayer: Record in your journal the thoughts and feelings that have surfaced during your prayer.

Jesus the Lord

Acts of the Apostles 1:6–11

> Now having met together, they asked me, "Lord, has the time come? Are you going to restore the kingdom to Israel?" He replied, "It is not for you to know times or dates that the Father has decided by his own authority, but you will receive power when the Holy Spirit comes on you, and then you will be my witnesses not only in Jerusalem but throughout Judea and Samaria, and indeed to the ends of the earth."

> As he said this he was lifted up while they looked on, and the cloud took him from their sight. They were still staring into the sky when suddenly two men in white were standing near them and they said, "Why are you men from Galilee standing here looking into the sky? Jesus who has been taken up from you into heaven, this same Jesus will come back in time same way as you have seen him go there."

Commentary:

It is not "Good-bye." It is "Welcome!"

The Ascension is a departure only in the sense that Jesus transcends spatiotemporal limitations, the restrictions of his historical physical presence. The Ascension, in effect, is welcoming us to share in his being present in a new way.

The Ascension and the Resurrection, although related, are two different events and play two different roles. During the past century, the development of the theology and liturgy of the Resurrection has been deepened and celebrated. This advancement has been a tremendous benefit for our contemporary spirituality.

Little attention has been given to the Ascension and it has been, for the most part, very misunderstood. When taken literally, the ascension is vulnerable to being dismissed. Unfortunately, we have been overly influenced by teachings and art that interpret the Ascension literally and inaccurately. The Ascension has not been depicted, either in language or in artistic forms that are metaphorically full or adequate. Beautiful though they are and as well intentioned as the artist may have been, stained glass windows of clouds with the feet of Jesus protruding simply do not convey the fullness of the mystery of the Ascension.

Fortunately, we are being blessed with tenacious scripture scholars who are opening for us the hidden treasure of the Ascension. For example, N. T. Wright's work on the Ascension makes clear the meaning of the Ascension and addresses the problems that serve as obstacles to the understanding and message of the Ascension.

Wright says one of the problems is with our concept and view of space. An inadequate, literal view sees space as a receptacle with a clear delineation of localities.

...theologians who take the Ascension seriously insist that it demands what some have called a relational view. Basically, heaven and earth in biblical cosmology are not two different locations within the same continuum of space or matter. They are two different dimensions of God's good creation. And the point about heaven is twofold.

First, heaven relates to earth tangentially so that the one who is in heaven can be present simultaneously anywhere and everywhere on earth: the Ascension therefore means that Jesus is available, accessible [to all people, everywhere, and at all times]. Second, heaven is, as it were, the control room for earth;...the place from which instructions are given. "All authority is given to me," said Jesus at the end of Matthew's gospel, "in heaven and on earth."
(Wright 2008, 114)

What good news! Jesus is not far away and earth and heaven are not two localities. It is almost unthinkable for us to view heaven and earth not as two distinct and separate locations but as two dimensions of the same world relating and interlocking. It is clearly a mystery, but just because we don't understand it all doesn't mean we cannot appreciate and glean the beauty and wisdom of these new insights and incorporate them into our own graced spirituality.

"The Ascension thus speaks of the Jesus who remains truly human and hence in an important sense absent from us while in another equally important sense present to us in a new way"

(Wright 2008, 116); he is free and accessible in the two dimensions of heaven and earth, and he is the Lord who directs the new order, the new world, the coming of fullness, the Kingdom!

To embrace the mystery of the Ascension is to breathe a sigh of relief; it is to give up being God. All obsessive, compulsive arrogant self-aggrandizement falls away. We relax and enjoy the reality that God is God, and we are creatures. And this gracious God has given us the Lord Jesus who reigns at the helm of the world. The Lord Jesus is interceding to the Father for us, laboring for us, and is already at work in our alienated, rebellious world, transforming, radically healing, and bringing all to justice.

The mission call of the Ascension is service. It is a call for our participation in this great work of Christ: "you will be my witnesses not only in Jerusalem but throughout Judea and Samaria, and indeed to the ends of the earth" (Acts 1:8).

Jesus the Lord is the leader, and we as his followers receive our direction and instruction from his Spirit "in whom we move and live and have our being" (Acts 17:28). It is in the power and leadership of the Lord Jesus that all things will be made new. The Lordship of Jesus trumps all other powers both earthly and heavenly.

> But God raised him high and gave him the name which is above all other names so that all beings in the heavens, on earth and in the underworld, shall bend the knee at the name of Jesus and that every tongue should acclaim Jesus Christ as Lord to the glory of God the Father. (Phil. 2:9–11)

Jesus the Lord

Suggested approach to prayer: On the Mountain

+ Daily prayer plan   (Orientations p. xxxi)

> I quiet myself and relax in the presence ofGod. I declare my dependency on God.

Grace: I beg for the gift of an intimate knowledge of a sharing of goods that God does in his love for me and how, at every moment and in every way, the many gifts of God inundate and surround me. Filled with gratitude, I desire to be empowered to respond just as totally in my love and service of God.

Method: Ignatian Contemplation   (Orientations p. xxxiv)

+ Reread the passage from Acts of the Apostles, and make it your own. Employing all your senses, be at the event of the Ascension.

> Image yourself present on the mountain outside Jerusalem with the disciples as they gather with Jesus. Be there with him; see what is happening as you enter into the dialog between the disciples and Jesus. How do you feel? What are your thoughts? Are you fearful?

> Watch him as he is gradually taken from their sight. Listen to the angels as they challenge your perception of his going away into the sky.

As you and the disciples make your way back to the upper room in Jerusalem, what do you talk about?

How are you challenged to meet the mystery of Christ's life, to seriously witness his presence as a way of life?

+ As the time of your prayer draws to a conclusion, spend twenty minutes in quiet contemplative prayer.

+ Close your prayer with an Our Father.

+ Review of Prayer: Record in your journal the thoughts and feeling that have surfaced during your prayer.

Jesus the Lord

Complimentary prayer: Narnia

In this prayer period, use the introductory and closing framework of the previous prayer

Method: Poetry as Prayer   (Orientations p. xxxix)

In the coming days, at your leisure, watch the movie *Narnia.*

Allow yourself to enter imaginatively in the story line. Accompany Peter, Susan, Edmond, and Lucy through the wardrobe door into Narnia.

Simply enjoy the movie.

After the movie, spend some time reflecting on the characters, story lines, and themes. Where did you find meanings that nurtured and enriched your soul?

Destined to Love

Acts 2:1–4

> When Pentecost day came round, they had all met in one room, when suddenly they heard what sounded like a powerful wind from heaven, the noise of which filled the entire house in which they were sitting, and something appeared to them that seemed like tongues of fire; these separated and came to rest on the head of each of them. They were all filled with the Holy Spirit and began to speak foreign languages as the Spirit gave them the gift of speech.

Commentary:

A kiss from God!

In the writings of the mystics and poets, the Holy Spirit has frequently been referred to as the kiss of God. "On the feast of Pentecost we celebrate the grace of being kissed by God" (Sanchez 2012, article).

To speak of the Spirit as the kiss of God is to speak of the incredible intimacy with which God gifts all creation. When kissed by God, the powerful breath and energy of God, the Spirit, flows into those consenting to and receiving the kiss. Each person who receives the gift of this kiss of the Spirit is enabled to recognize the Spirit as coming from the Lord and is empowered, in turn, to share that kiss with others. This new life, this empowerment and enablement, all comes from the Spirit. Once again, God the Creator, in the powerful breath of the Spirit, breathes new life into all of creation (Gen. 2:7b).

For the nascent Christian community, the coming of the Spirit is a towering miracle of the power of God. The disciples had returned from the mountain of the Ascension and gathered with other followers of Jesus in the upper room in Jerusalem. They joined in continuous prayer as they waited for the fulfillment of the promise of Jesus that he would send his Spirit. When the Spirit came, it came suddenly as mighty wind and tongues of fire that rested on each one of them. Immediately they began to speak in foreign languages.

The radical universal nature of the promised gift of the Spirit compelled the early community to go into the streets of Jerusalem where people "from every nation under heaven were gathered for the Jewish feast of Pentecost" (Act 2:5), gathered to celebrate the giving of the Law on Mount Sinai. As members of the new Spirit-filled community spoke, the people who heard them were amazed. For, though the followers of Jesus were speaking Galilean, each of the listeners heard them in their own language.

Babel was reversed! (Gen. 11:1–9). With the coming of the Spirit, the new Law of love superseded the old Law mediated by Moses. To those who listened and believed, the new Spirit-filled community offered new life, new hope, and new power as they proclaimed Jesus as Lord.

Today, here and now, the Spirit of Pentecost continues to breathe forth on all humankind, and the same new life, hope, and power is available to us "if only we are willing to draw near and experience the kiss of the Spirit of our God" (Sanchez 2012, article).

The Spirit of Pentecost transforms those who trust and obey and seals them in the new covenant and community of love. They become people who seek their direction from the Lord Jesus who invites them, enfolds them, assures, and equips them for their task as participants in his mission.

The lifestyle that flows from being graced by the kiss of the Spirit at Pentecost celebrates and embodies the new covenant of love. The mandate arising from the grace of Pentecost insists on a renewal of mind and heart, a renewal grounded not in arbitrary and out-of-date rules but an ethics of holiness and justice best demonstrated in the teaching of Paul. "If I give away all that I possess piece by piece, and if I even let them take my body to burn it, but am without love, it will do me no good whatever...there are three things that last: faith, hope, and love; and the greatest of these is love" (1 Cor. 13:3, 13).

Underlying all that the Good News says about love is the command and commitment to forgive. It is essential not to close our hearts to forgiving those who, in ways large and small, betray us. Insofar as we refuse to forgive others, we cut ourselves off from receiving forgiveness, and as a result we live our lives in sadness filled with resentment and alienation.

As lovely as the poetic reading from 1 Corinthians is, it does not simply give us a rule of life but rather it recognizes our yearning to be more loving people. We are all aware of our human condition in which we fail in our loving and are incomplete. "For our knowledge is imperfect and our prophesying is imperfect; but once perfection comes all imperfect things will disappear...Now we are seeing a dim reflection in a mirror; but then we shall be seeing face to face. The knowledge that I have now is imperfect; but then I shall know as fully as I am known" (1 Cor. 13:9–10, 12). "The point of 1 Corinthians 13 is that love is not our duty; it is our *destiny*. It is the language Jesus spoke, and we are called to speak it so that we can converse with him. It is the food they eat in God's new world, and we must acquire the taste for it here and now. It is the music God has written for all his creatures to sing, and we are called to learn it and practice it now, so as to be ready when the conductor brings down his baton...Love is at the very heart of the surprise of hope: people who truly hope as the Resurrection encourages us to hope will be people enabled to love in a new way". (Wright 2008, 288).

So in the end, it is only Spirit; it is only love!

Destined to Love

Suggested approach to prayer: Gathered in the Spirit

+ Daily prayer plan   (Orientations p. xxxi)

  I quiet myself and relax in the presence ofGod. I declare
  my dependency on God.

Grace: I beg for the gift of an intimate knowledge of the sharing
of goods that God does for me and how in every moment and
in every way the many gifts of God's love inundate and surround
me. Filled with gratitude, I desire to be empowered to respond
just as totally in my love and service of God.

Method: Ignatian Contemplation   (Orientations p. xxxiv)

Prayerfully read Acts 2:1–4.

Image yourself as one of the disciples who returns from the
mountain of the Ascension. See yourself, with the others, climb-
ing the stairs to the Upper Room.

+ What are your memories as you enter this room where you
have spent time with Jesus and the other apostles?

+ What are your feelings as you recall the time on the mountain
and Jesus's instruction to return to Jerusalem. Fear? Anticipation?

Look at the faces of those gathered with you: the other apostles, Mary, some of the women disciples, and some other of Jesus's followers.

+ What do you say to each other?

+ How do you wait for the promise of Jesus—in conversation, in silence, in prayer?

Suddenly there is a sound like the sound of thunder, and then of a great wind. And you experience what seems like tongues of fire descending over each one.

+ Image the flame moving over you, entering into you. Be aware of the movements within your heart and mind.

Let yourself rest in the Gift of Jesus's own Spirit alive and burning within your heart.

+ As the time of your prayer draws to a conclusion, spend twenty minutes in quiet contemplative prayer.

+ Close your prayer with an Our Father.

+ Review of Prayer: Record in your journal the thoughts and feeling that have surfaced during your prayer.

Destined to Love

Complimentary prayer: Spirit of Wisdom, Spirit of Love

In this prayer period, use the introductory and closing framework of the previous prayer.

Prayerfully read the following quotations from the book of Wisdom (7:7, 22–30, 8:1) and St. Paul's First Letter to the Corinthians (1 Cor. 12:31, 13:4–8).

Consider the gifts of the Spirit that Wisdom describes as present within you. Ask the Spirit to effect in you, in your words, and deeds, the instruction of Paul.
I prayed, and understanding was given me;
I entreated, and the spirit of Wisdom came to me.

Be ambitious for the higher gifts. I am going to show you a way that is better than any of them.

...within her is a spirit
intelligent, holy, unique,
manifold, subtle, active,
incisive, unsullied,
invulnerable, benevolent,
sharp, irresistible,
beneficent, loving,
steadfast, dependable,
unperturbed.

Love *is* always patient and
kind; it is never jealous;
love is never boastful or
conceited.

almighty, all-surveying,
penetrating all intelligent,
pure and most
subtle spirits;
for Wisdom is quicker to
move than any motion;
she is so pure,
she pervades and
permeates all things.

Love is never rude or selfish;
it does not take offence,
and is not resentful.

She is a breath of the
power of God,
pure emanation of the
glory of the Almighty;
hence nothing impure
can find a way into her.
She is a reflection of
the eternal light,
untarnished mirror of
God's active power,
image of his goodness.

Love takes no pleasure
in other people's sins but
delights in the truth.

Although alone, she can do all things;
herself unchanging, she
makes all things new.
In every generation she
passes into holy souls,
she makes them friends of
God and prophets;
for God loves only the one
who lives with Wisdom.

Love is always ready to
excuse, to trust, to hope,
and to endure whatever
comes.

She is indeed more
splendid than the sun,
she outshines all the constellations;
compared with light, she
takes first place,
for light must yield to night,
but over Wisdom evil
can never triumph.

> Love does not come to an
> end.

She deploys her strength from one
end of the earth to the other,
ordering all things for good.

Repetition Day: God pours forth himself in all the gifts that he showers upon us.

Grace: I beg for the gift of an intimate knowledge of the sharing of goods that God does in his love for me, and how, at every moment and in every way, the many gifts of God's love inundate and surround me. Filled with gratitude, I want to be empowered to respond just as totally in my love and service of God.

Approach to prayer: Repetition   (Orientations p. xlii)

In preparation, I review my prayer by rereading my journal of the past days. I select for my repetition the period of prayer that most revealed to me an awareness of deep communion with God, and in which I was moved by joy, amazement, gratitude, and awe. I proceed in the manner I did originally, focusing on the scene, word, or feeling that was previously most significant. I may choose to return to a passage with which I had difficulty.

I consider how, like any reasonable person, I am moved to respond to this God who invites me to deep union and communion with him and all creation. Moved by love, I may find that I can best respond in the words of the following prayer of St. Ignatius:

> Take, Lord, and receive all my liberty, my memory, my understanding, and my entire will—all that I have and call my own. You have given it all to me. To you, Lord, I return it. Everything is yours; do with it what you will. Give me only your love and your grace. That is enough for me.

Review of prayer: I write in my journal any feelings, experiences, or insights that have come to my awareness with a particular significance during this prayer.

Point 6

Take Lord and Receive

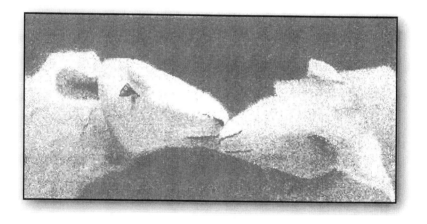

What Is My Response to so Great a Lover?

Take, Lord, and receive all my liberty, my memory, my understanding, and my entire will—all that I have and call my own. You have given it all to me. To you, Lord, I return it. Everything is yours; do with it what you will.

Give me only your love and your grace. That is enough for me.

Your Kingdom Come

Matthew 6:10

> Your kingdom come…

Commentary:

> It was the best of times, it was the worst of times, it was the age of wisdom, it was the age of foolishness, it was epoch of belief, it was epoch of incredulity, it was the season of Light, it was the season of Darkness, it was the spring of hope, it was the winter of despair…

This introduction to *A Tale of Two Cities* could well serve as an editorial in the present-day *New York Times*.

It could also serve as a description of the history of Israel. Always, the people of God have walked within paradox as they struggled with the reality of the frailty of their human condition. Only in their heartfelt remembering of the promises of the prophets were they able to endure the suffering that was part of ongoing political upheaval, exile, and societal breakdown. In the midst of nearly overwhelming distress, the voice of Ezekiel sustained their hope.

> I am going to take you from among the nations and gather you all together from all the foreign countries, and bring you home to your own land…I shall give you a new heart,

and put a new spirit in you…You shall be my people and I will be your God. (Ezek. 36:24, 26, 28)

The Jewish people lived out of the conviction that God would vindicate Israel by destroying evil and bringing about a new heaven and a new earth. It was God's task to fulfill his promise.

With the coming of Jesus, the promise of Ezekiel takes on an immanent fullness. "The time has come, and the kingdom of God is close at hand. Repent, and believe the Good News" (Mark 1:15).

For Jesus, the kingdom of God meant "that God turns to human beings totally and without any reservations to bring divine abundance to the world" (Lohfink 2012, 220).

Joseph Ratzinger speaks of this abundance as the "law of excess or superfluity." He says that Jesus "is the righteousness of God which goes beyond what need be, which does not calculate, which really overflows; the not 'withstanding' of his greater love, in which he infinitely surpasses the failing efforts of man" (Lohfink 2012, 243). Like the seller of grain who always gives "a good measure, pressed down, mounded over, even pouring an excess into the buyer's apron, love is always love without measure, love overflowing" (Luke 6:38).

> Superfluity, wealth, and extravagant luxury are thus the sign of the day of salvation—not skimpiness, meagerness, wretchedness, and need. Why? Because God's very self is overflowing life and because God longs to give a share

in that life. God's love is without measure; God does not give to human beings according to the measure of their good behavior or service. (Lohfink 2012, 243–44)

No wonder the Gospel is filled with joyous occasions of banquets and weddings!

For Jesus, the reign of God is not projected into some far away future. He speaks of it in the present as he prays, "your kingdom come." The reign of God is visible in Jesus as he heals the crippled and the blind, frees those held captive, exorcises demons, comforts those who mourn, and "binds up hearts that are broken" (Isa. 61:1–3). Jesus manifested the Kingdom of God through the enlightened radiance of his goodness that set the human heart ablaze and released the root of love into the world—revealing the very heart of God's presence. (Bourgeault 2013, 181).

Primary among the deeds of Jesus and from the very beginning, he began to gather a community of disciples around him. Jesus gave the disciples a new way of being together.

"He…brings them around a table, and practices with them the table customs of the reign of God: that one should not choose the best place but instead wait to see what place one is given; that the one who wants to be first must be the servant of all; that disciples should wash each other's feet, just as he has done—that is do the dirty work for others; that disciples must forgive each other seventy-seven times, that is, always and without ceasing; and that they should look out not for the splinter in a sister's or a brother's eye". (Lohfink 2012, 353)

Jesus never called his disciples to human perfection, but only to the perfection of undivided surrender to the will of God, in constant conversion and reconciliation.

Finally, Jesus shared with his nascent community his own prayer, "Your kingdom come."

With hearts on fire, they were set ablaze with the passion of Christ. His mission became their own. They experienced the kingdom as palpable and visible, and that they, with Jesus, had a part to play in its actualization. With great joy and devotion, they were impelled to sacrifice everything for this great cause.

We, in our time, are invited to follow the path of the first disciples, to open our hearts to receive the fullness of God's love and to energetically embrace the mission of Christ.

> ...the energy of our devotion becomes a point of light within the world. At the present time a map is being unfolded made of the lights of the lovers of God. The purpose of this map is to change the inner energy structure of the planet. In previous ages this energy structure was held by sacred places, stone circles, temples and cathedrals. In the next stage of our collective evolution it is the hearts of individuals that will hold the cosmic note of the planet. This note can be recognized as a song being infused into the hearts of seekers. It is a quality of joy that is being infused into the world. It is the heartbeat of the world and needs to be heard in our cities and towns.
> (L. Vaughan-Lee, quoted in Bourgeault 2013, 180)

Your Kingdom Come

Suggested approach to prayer: The Body of Christ

+ Daily prayer plan   (Orientations p. xxxi)

I quiet myself and relax in the presence of God. I declare my dependency on God.

Grace: I beg for the gift that henceforth I will consciously and intentionally live in the Spirit of Jesus, so that with St. Paul I can say, "I live now, not I, but Christ" (Gal. 2:20).

Method: Poetry as Prayer   (Orientations p. xxxiv)

We awaken in Christ's
body as Christ awakens our
bodies, and my poor hand
is Christ.
He enters my foot, and is infinitely me.

I move my hand, and wonderfully
my hand becomes Christ, becomes all of
Him (for God is indivisibly
whole, seamless in his Godhood)

I move my foot, and at once
he appears like a flash of lightning.
Do my words seem blasphemous?—
Then open your heart to Him.

and let yourself receive the one who is
opening to you so deeply.
For if we genuinely love Him,
we wake up inside Christ's body.

where all our body, all over
every most hidden *part* of it,

is realized in joy as Him,
and He makes us utterly real.

and everything that is hurt,
everything that seemed to us dark,
harsh, shameful, maimed, ugly,
irreparably
damaged, is in Him transformed.

and recognized as
whole, as lovely, and
radiant in His light.
We awaken as the Beloved in every part of our body.
                    (Symeon, the New Theologian, 949–1022)

+ As the time of your prayer draws to a conclusion, spend twenty minutes in contemplative prayer.

+ Close your prayer with an Our Father.

+ Review of prayer: Record in your journal the thoughts and feelings that have surfaced during your prayer.

Repetition Day: The Contemplatio as a Way of Life

Grace: I beg for the gift that henceforth I will consciously and intentionally live in the Spirit of Jesus, so that with St. Paul I can say, "I live now, not I, but Christ" (Gal. 2:20).

Approach to prayer: (Orientations p. xlii)

In preparation, I review my prayer by rereading my journal. I select for my repetition the period of prayer that most compels me to a total surrender of myself to the person and mission of Christ.

I consider how, like any reasonable person, I am moved to respond in love using of the words of St. Ignatius:

> Take, Lord, and receive all my liberty, my memory, my understanding, and my entire will—all that I have and call my own. You have given it all to me.
>
> To you, Lord, I return it. Everything is yours; do with it what you will. Give me only your love and your grace. That is enough for me.

Appendix A

Ignatian Practices

Two Standards

Three Kinds of Persons

Three Kinds of Humility

TWO STANDARDS

> There was a little girl,
> Who had a little curl
> Right in the middle of her forehead
> When she was good
> She was very good indeed,
> And when she was bad she was horrid.

> (HENRY WADSWORTH LONGFELLOW)

The choice for the good or the not so good or even the horrid is a challenge right from the beginning!

Many of us can recall the sound of our mother's voice as she chanted out this rhyme, sometimes as an encouragement toward good behavior but most frequently as a reprimand for our not so good behavior.

It is pleasant to imagine that as we moved toward maturity we effortlessly grew in becoming "very good indeed"; however, the complications of our human condition and our freedom to choose presents a radically different reality. Fortunately, we make many wonderful and good choices that bring us and those we love peace and happiness. Our choices for good contribute to the well-being of our world. However, there is another path in which we make unfortunate choices that have the potential for incredible pain and suffering. The childhood behaviors that were not so good and perhaps seemingly horrid have the capacity to move from small acts of rebellion and possessiveness to

enticements and temptations in which we can become danger-
ously entrapped.

The writings of Vatican II remind us that

> Man...is divided in himself. As a result, the whole life of
> people, both individual and social, shows itself to be a
> struggle and a dramatic one, between good and evil,
> between light and darkness. People find that they are
> unable of themselves to overcome the assaults of evil
> successfully so that everyone feels as though bound by
> chains. But the Lord himself came to free and strengthen
> his people, renewing them inwardly and casting out the
> "ruler of this world," (John 12:31) who held him in the
> bondage of sin.
> (W. Abbot 1966, 13)

As Christians we are called, with Christ, to face this division within us, this struggle of good and evil, and to make the choices in
which we participate in advancing the kingdom of God.

Although the power of evil is not equal to the force and power
of good, the presence of darkness is a blatant reality and can be
a pervasive presence. It may be very seductive, even appearing,
at first, as light, as a good choice. It is not easy to recognize the
subtlety of darkness; its entrapment can be gradual. It appeals to
our natural human desire to possess, to be accepted, approved,
and praised, to be safe and secure. We are "broadsided" in our
humanness. There is within all of us areas of weakness and in-
completeness. This is where we are most vulnerable and blind to

the subtlety of the enticements of darkness. Paul acknowledged this reality when he said: "I do not do what I want, but I do the very thing I hate" (Rom. 7:15).

Making enlightened life-giving choices requires astute self-awareness and a discipline of prayerful discernment. St. Ignatius offers us a reflective process, a series of contemplations known as the Two Standards in which one is empowered to recognize the strategies and tactics of the evil one as well a deepening appreciation of Jesus and how he calls us to participate with him in service of the kingdom. Once one has committed oneself to Christ, one is less apt to yield to blatant evil. However, one needs to continue throughout Life to be aware of the subtle temptations that can sabotage one's choice to place oneself under the banner, the standard of Christ.

The grace one is to request when praying the Two Standards is for the knowledge to be able to detect the strategies of Satan and to beg for help against the particular tactics of evil to which one is most vulnerable. At the same time, one also asks for the knowledge of true life in Christ in order to be able to follow the pattern of Christ's life and to make all one's decisions in light of his way.

The contemplations of the Two Standards "draws on the deep power of myth, vividly contrasting the characters of Christ and Lucifer in cosmic confrontation. The text describes a concrete place, complete with graphic imagery and imaginative design. Yet this cosmic struggle echoes within each person and a world marked by the continuing struggle between truth and deception" (Dyckman, Garvin, and Liebert 1989, 194).

The first movement into the exercise is to see before oneself, at opposite poles, Christ and Satan. We see Christ extending an invitation to us to join him in his life and mission and we see Satan, with his minions, enticing us to his side.

In illustrating the confrontation, Ignatius has divided the contemplation into two parts.

In the first part, Satan is imaged sitting on his throne in the center of the city of Babylon. The direction is to imagine the scene. See Satan as he is surrounded by fire and smoke and then image how he might look; contriving, snarling, and so on. He sends out demons, disguised, throughout the whole world to every country, to every town, to every home, and to each individual. Satan tells them to cast out their nets and be ready to chain those they tempt to riches, honor, and pride.

In the second part, we see Christ within the city of peace. Ignatius has us imagine the beauty of this place, the quiet gentleness of undisturbed nature and Christ sitting among his followers. Jesus adopts a strategy that is just the opposite of Satan: He sends his followers throughout the world instructing them in the ways of love, peace, and freedom. They are to "help people not enslave or oppress them… [and to] attract men and women to the highest spiritual poverty, and should it please God, and should he draw them to want to choose it, even to a life of actual poverty. Being poor, they will be led to accept and even to desire the insults and contempt of the world. The result will be a life of true humility" (Fleming 1980, 87–89).

The Two Standards leads us to confront each of the conflicting poles while encountering the three major choices one faces within the circumstances of their life; to choose poverty over riches, dishonor over honor, and humility rather than pride.

The prayer of the Two Standards has the potential to radically transform an individual. "The Two Standards unmasks every person's need for God and the cost of choosing to follow Jesus. This discernment leads to a greater commitment which Ignatius recognized by the presence of the three virtues: poverty rather than riches, reproaches or contempt rather than honor, and humility rather than pride" (Dyckman, Garvin, and Lebert 1989, 196).

"Very good indeed."

(Spiritual Exercises: Paragraphs 136-148)

THREE KINDS OF PERSONS

The Spiritual Exercises: Paragraph 149–157

In the second week of the Exercises, Ignatius invites the retreatant to reflect on and to grow in an awareness of the attitudes that underlie our use of the gifts that have been entrusted to us. It is a simple reflection and invitation to examine and to ask to be freed of the attachments we have, even to what is good.

In the reflection in the Exercises, Ignatius uses the example of three persons—all of whom wish to save their souls—who have received a large sum of money. The money represents any gift or talent one has. It might be a relationship, a position, a family inheritance, and the like. It is precious to us; we cherish it.

One begins with the realization that whatever this one thing is, it is a gift, given freely to us. It is a good that is part of our lives. And whatever that good is, the underlying desire of our hearts is to use it for the glory and service of God.

The first person becomes enamored with the money; he loves being wealthy. He enjoys the prestige and security wealth has brought to him. He handles his business affairs with the utmost integrity. At the same time, he is aware of the effects the attachment is having on him. As he puts his money into those investments that are the most profitable, he becomes progressively preoccupied with the returns he receives. He senses that something is amiss. He tells himself that someday, somehow, he will come to terms with this nagging voice within. The "someday" never comes. Without ever realizing what his inner voice was inviting him to enjoy, the man dies.

The second person also becomes fascinated with her newly acquired wealth. However, from the beginning, she has a keen awareness of the ramifications of such wealth. She is especially concerned that her attachment does not prove to be detrimental to her relationship with God. She finds herself in a dilemma. On the one hand, she wants to be free of her infatuation with this money, and on the other hand, she certainly does not want to lose control of this gift. She reaches the decision that it would please God if she were to do something truly wonderful for others with the interest on the money. So she decides to use a percentage of the money earned to build a new library for the community in which she lives. The building is impressive; on the cornerstone is inscribed not only the date but her name as principal benefactor. The third person, too, is concerned about how best to make use of this large amount of money. His question is: How can I best use this gift to reflect the pure goodness of God? He wants to do with the money only what God wants him to do. Though he has no idea what that means specifically, he is confident that God will show him the way. So, at peace with this assurance, he secures the money in a trust fund to be used at the time when the direction will be clear. At the same time, he makes a firm promise to nurture within himself an openness to God through prayer and to develop a sensitivity to the needs of others who might benefit by the trust fund.

Ignatius invites us to ponder the parable as we reflect on the gifts that we have been given, those things especially that have special hold on us. All too easily we may take them for granted and not examine the attitudes that shape our way of making use of them.

A way of approaching this reflection would be to prayerfully reflect, making use of the following questions:

+ What are the gifts or "riches" that have been given to me?

+ How are my responses similar or dissimilar to those of the first person? The second person?

The third person?

In an attempt to become more aware of the disorder in my attachments, and how they may be an obstacle to my total surrender to God, I consider questions like the following:

+ What do my fears concerning loss tell me about what I cling to (e.g., loss of status and reputation)?

+ Where in my life do I most frequently hear my voice of conscience, affirming, prodding, nagging me?

+ What are those things, good in themselves, which tend to enslave me because of my attitude toward them?

+ What are the areas of unfreedom in the use of my gifts? How, even as I use them for good, I am certain to remain in control?

+ Where do I most experience the peace and freedom of being so totally attached to Christ that I can "take or leave" any particular thing, advantage, or honor?

Becoming aware of the obstacles to the total surrender to God takes a long time and is not easy. Once we make this discovery, Ignatius suggests that we take to prayer the very thing to which we are overly attached and ask God to remove it from us if it is truly God's will that we do not have that particular form of "riches." This radical and even painful prayer is a means of transforming one's attitude from the consideration of the "riches" as "mine" to the realization that all is gift from God.

(An adaptation, taken from Bergan and Schwan 1985, 71–73)

THE THREE KINDS OF HUMILITY

The Spiritual Exercises: Paragraph 164–168

In the second week of the Exercises, St. Ignatius offers the retreatant a meditation, akin to the Principle and Foundation, in that it is not a formal exercise of prayer, but rather an invitation to reflect and make one's own Ignatius's insight into the predisposition for a generous response to Christ.

There are, he says, "three kinds" of humility. The first, necessary for salvation, is a stance of accepting fully the fact that one is a creature, totally dependent upon the Creator. Simply put, one would do nothing to fracture the relationship with God, that is, to commit a serious, mortal, sin.

The second, "more perfect than the first" consists in the same indifference, the same preference of God's service and praise above all other things as is found in the Principle and Foundation.

> In this second kind of humility, submission to the will of God, desire for God's service and glory, has become so centrally the focus of the human creature's will that even minor inconsistencies in our choices—expressions of unbalanced desire for our own pleasure, security, or self-advancement—cease to operate. (Daily1995, 27)

The third kind of humility, presupposing the first and second kinds of humility, consists in this:

I so much want the truth of Christ's life to be fully the truth of my own that I find myself, moved by grace, with a love and a desire for poverty in order to be with the poor Christ; a love and a desire for insults in order to be closer to Christ in *his* own rejection by people; a love and a desire to be considered worthless and a fool for Christ, rather than to be esteemed as wise and prudent according to the standards of Christ. By grace, I find myself so moved to follow Jesus Christ in the most intimate union possible, that his experiences are reflected in my own. (Fleming 1980, #167, 103)

If this third kind of humility seems somewhat forbidding or at the very least, daunting, it is important to note that the third degree of humility as Ignatius envisions it, is more a question of desire, of preference rather than of behavior. One does not arbitrarily place oneself in a situation of the third kind of humility. It is always a gift and grace at the initiative of God.

In his book, *Spiritual Freedom*, John English, SJ, sees a parallel between the three kinds of humility and the commitment and love between a husband and wife. In effect, they say to each other:

+ I will always be faithful to you to the extent of never committing adultery.

+ I will avoid all disturbances with you in the sense that I will always try to be at peace with you and try to be an instrument of peace within the family.

+ I will feel with you; I will suffer with you in your sufferings; I will be joyful with you in your joy. I would be with you even in failure (Fleming 1980,172).

Seen from the perspective of a marriage covenant, one can understand how, for Ignatius and his companions, to speak of choosing humility with Christ was clearly a way of speaking about love.

As one comes to know and love Christ, a desire to "put on his mind and heart" grows apace. The description of the third kind of humility describes the self-emptying of Jesus that reveals the incredible love of God for his creatures (Phil. 2:5–11).

> ...choosing to be formed with Christ is really the heart of Christian faith...our submission to his will, always is finally expressed not in the "ascent" of achievement so much as in the "descent" of a similar self-emptying in which we experience the transcendence beyond ourselves into the mystery of God. (B. Daley, 1995, 33)

As I ponder these three kinds of humility, what evidence do I find of each within myself as I seek to be ever more fully a disciple of Christ and to bring, in his spirit, the love of God to our world? Am I free enough to pray for the totally selfless love of the third kind of humility if it is God's *will* for me?

Father Medaille expresses beautifully the heart of the third kind of humility as he prays:

It seems to me, good Jesus, that, at the moment of your Incarnation, God your Father or your holy angels might possibly have indicated to you that you were about to lay yourself open to excessive pain for the sake of creatures far too unworthy of it and that your love urged you to reply that, whatever might be the cost to you, you wanted to save them. In gratitude for such great goodness ought I not likewise say that whatever might be the cost to me, good Jesus, I want to be wholly yours, and even if at every moment, out of love for you, I must endure sufferings as great and trying as those you were pleased to endure for me. (Medaille, S.J. Maxims of Perfection II 1978,6)

Appendix B

Contemplative Practice

Centering Prayer—Contemplative Prayer
Welcoming Prayer

CENTERING PRAYER–CONTEMPLATIVE PRAYER

"It is the Spirit who prays in us." (Rom. 8:26)

It ought to come as no surprise that a book based on the Contemplation to Attain the Love of God—the crown of the Spiritual Exercises—has as its major focus to entice and guide the reader into contemplative prayer. The suggestions for prayer invite the one who prays into that deep and intimate relational space between the Lover and the Beloved.

God is always gift and giver—love and loving.

God dwells within us as the very love-ground of our being. We, with all of creation, from the beginning of time, have been yearning for the fulfillment of our true selves within this loving presence. The Spirit gives prayerful voice to this desire and calls everything into full participation with God's self. God's very Spirit prays for us, within us. Yielding to that Divine reality, all of creation is united in joy.

Contemplative prayer gifts us with the grace of receptivity to this love presence. It is saying yes to God's gift of God's Divine self within us. Within this pure gift of sacred receptivity, our consciousness is gradually awakened to the deeper reality of God's being that already exists within us. We are brought, through the gracious goodness of God, to the "discovery of our true personhood in union with God, other people and all of creation."

The living tradition of contemplative prayer comes to us through God's movement of prayer within the hearts of our desert mothers and fathers. In the fourth century, God brought forth a new understanding of how to radically give oneself to God. A great shift occurred. "Becoming a martyr and dying at the hands of Roman persecution in witness for Christ changed into becoming a 'martyr of conscience' and dying an interior death into the inner resurrection of the contemplative life" (Keating 2008,10).

The desert Abbas and Ammas embraced the new vision of losing one's life in order to find it (Matt. 10:39). Generations followed in their footsteps. Communities that were committed to living out the contemplative dimension of the Gospel were formed and provided the foundation for monastic contemplative life. The Spirit of God was uniquely expressed in each generation and each built on the previous generation's contemplative experience and growth.

God has continued to foster this movement of contemplative prayer, and we are witnesses to its renewal in our time. Thomas Merton, a Trappist Monk, writing in the 1960s, was instrumental in raising the awareness of contemplative prayer to those living outside the monastery. His writings on contemplative spirituality were timely and enthusiastically received; they gifted the Church with a new impetus to the practice of contemplative prayer. His works continue to provide hope and inspiration to ordinary people yearning to discover a deeper relationship with God. His legacy of wisdom to God's people has been profound:

he has gifted us with the firm foundation of an emphasis on contemplative prayer that is oriented toward integrating the divine and the human—seeing God in all things. It was he who used the term "center" to symbolize that concentrated point within us where life springs from God. He reemphasized the basic Gospel premise that effective action flows from prayer. The work of social justice activities should not be considered separate from the contemplative life.

From the time of Merton, many spiritual masters of contemplative prayer followed, and they have contributed significantly to the renewal of contemplative practice in recent history.

Extraordinary among them is Trappist Monk, Thomas Keating. He was deeply touched by the spiritual hunger he experienced in people and was moved by a prophetic call to respond. He raised the question to his fellow monks; "Is it not possible to put the essence of Christian contemplative path into a meditation method accessible to modem people living in the world?" This question stirred the heart of his fellow monk William Meninger who, by drawing on the instructions given in the spiritual classic, *The Cloud of the Unknowing*, founded the method of Centering Prayer (Bourgeault 2004, 57).

It was rather like a "Pentecost" happening—the flame of contemplative prayer spread one to another and a powerful movement ensued. Largely through the efforts of Thomas Keating, an international membership network, Contemplative Outreach, was formed, which offers the teaching and practice of Centering Prayer. Today, thousands of people have an established practice of Centering Prayer. Through the dedication of holy men and women, the contemplative practice has been rediscovered with renewed vitality in our contemporary time.

The method of Centering Prayer, which is considered the path to contemplative prayer, is simple. Simplicity is not necessarily easy and quick. Centering Prayer, which leads one toward transformation in Christ, requires patient attentiveness and the discipline of consistent practice.

The method of Centering Prayer proposed by Father Menninger is based primarily on what he learned in chapter seven from *The Cloud of Unknowing*:

So whenever you feel drawn by grace to the contemplative work and are determined to do it, simply raise your heart to God with a gentle stirring of love. Think only of God, the God who created you, redeemed you, and guided you to this work. Allow no other ideas about God to enter your mind. Yet even this is too much. A naked intent toward God, the desire for him alone, is enough.

If you want to gather all your desire into one simple word that the mind can easily retain, choose a short word rather than a long one. A one-syllable word such as "God" or "love" is best. But choose one that is meaningful to you. Then fix it in your mind so that it will remain there come what way (Johnston 1973, 56).

These words from *The Cloud of the Unknowing* became the cornerstone for the basic guidelines taught by Thomas Keating and Contemplative Outreach:

1. Choose a sacred word as the symbol of your intention to consent to God's presence and action within.
2. Sitting comfortably and with eyes closed, settle briefly and silently introduce the sacred word as the symbol of your consent to God's presence and action within.
3. When engaged with your thoughts (which include body sensations, feelings, images, and reflections) return ever so gently to the sacred word.
4. At the end of the prayer period, remain in silence with eyes closed for a couple of minutes. (Frenette 2012, 6)

In his book, *Open Mind, Open Heart* (Keating 1997), Keating teaches that one may, instead of a sacred word, use other forms to express your consent to God's presence. This might be the use of your breath or a glance. Another way is to enter into the practice without a symbol, through a sacred nothingness. Though the ways of practicing with these different symbols are similar, however, one may experience different benefits as different symbols can assist you in expressing where you might be in the particular season of your spiritual journey (Frenette 2012, 24). Keating also calls us to remember the essential intent of Centering Prayer is receptivity. He cautions that this is attained only through a gentle attitude toward oneself and in the way and manner one disposes one's self to prayer. We are assured that gradually the contemplative attitudes of gentleness, letting go and resting develop not only in prayer but also in our external lifestyle. The grace of Centering Prayer moves us into a new way of being.

Centering prayer is a beautiful path, and as one's practice evolves in a natural manner, an awareness grows that the sacred word arises from the mind of God, and from one's prayer, and then moves more deeply into what could be termed "classic contemplative." At this point of awareness, one lets go of the sacred word in order that one may be able to rest in God's sacred word.

Thomas Keating's empowering teachings calls us to say yes not only to God's presence within us but also to God's action that includes purification and transformation (Frenette 2012, 14).

He teaches that although we are not separate from God. We are born into the human condition and in spite of the fundamental goodness of human nature, we experience life's inevitable harshness. We all have been damaged in various ways, in varying degrees by circumstances such as poverty, war, neglect, abuse, grief, and loss. Some of our emotional harm may have come from those to whom our care was entrusted or it may have arisen as a consequence of our own actions. Whatever the cause of our emotional wounding, it initiates, within our psychological framework, compensatory mechanisms that can serve as obstacles to our intentional reception of God's love and action within us. For example, due to not being affectionately cared for in childhood, one may throughout one's entire life spend enormous amounts of energy in order to attain approval and esteem. Or, for instance, because one has lacked stability in our childhood one may spend an entire life gathering possessions and acquisitions to ensure security. These patterns of compulsive and addictive behaviors draw us away from our focus on God within, and distance us from God's holy intention for us.

Thomas Keating describes this process as the formation and consequent need to dismantle the false self. His teachings on contemplative prayer assures us that the regular practice of contemplative prayer not only makes us aware of the life destructiveness of false self-behaviors but exposes us to the healing transformative action of God in which we are purified of such behaviors and discover our true selves in God. Keating calls this process of radical personal transformation divine therapy and refers to God as the Divine Therapist. In the self-gifting of God in contemplative prayer, we are freed in God.

Frenette expresses the development of "contemplative prayer as a paradox, it is love, non-dual love, pure love. At the edge of pure contemplation, by letting everything be, just as it is, in God, one is 'practicing' love, pure love" (Frenette 2012, 97).

Frenette cites Merton's expression of this mysterious paradox. When the next step comes, you do not take the step…what happens is that the separate entity that is you apparently disappears and nothing seems to be left but a pure freedom indistinguishable from infinite Freedom, love identified with Love. Not two loves, one waiting for the other…and here, is where contemplation becomes what it is Truly meant to be, it is no longer something infused by God into a created subject, so much as God living in God, and identifying a created life with His own Life so there is nothing left of any significance but God living in God (Merton 2003,289–90).

Centering prayer/contemplative prayer offers a harmonious compliment to the Ignatian exercise, the Contemplation to Attain

Divine Love. In the exercise we are asked to meditate and to consider what would be an appropriate response to the greatest Lover who has given us so much. Ignatius writes: "Love consists in interchange between two parties; that is to say in the lover's giving and communicating to the beloved what he has or out of what he has or can; and so, on the contrary, the beloved to the lover. The same of honors, of riches and so the one to the other." (Fleming 1996, 174).

In his own time, Ignatius absorbed and integrated practices of prayer that were current in his own time, and those who knew him, saw in him a profound mysticism in his awareness of the pervading presence of God and his seeking and finding God in all things. So today, "in the seeking of wisdom from different paradigms of prayer, the Spirit is allowed freedom to move one's heart to a greater receptivity to Divine Love" (Wilder 2013, Presence Magazine, Vol.19, No.2, June, 52-60).

WELCOMING PRAYER

Welcoming Prayer is Centering Prayer's powerful companion piece, "its tool par excellence" for grounding and bridging the practice of centering prayer with the activities of our daily life. It is a practice of prayer that "turns our daily life into a virtually limitless field for inner awakening" (Bourgeault 2004, 135).

God called you out of the darkness into his wonderful light.

The graces of the Welcoming prayer release us into God's merciful light that frees us from distortions that hinder our path to fullness of life in God. Welcoming prayer is a discipline of prayer that sheds light on behaviors that have unconsciously developed in order to compensate for deprivation of instinctual needs in childhood and/or debilitating life circumstances. This process of developing compensatory behaviors is what Thomas Keating calls the creation of the "Homemade Self" or False Self.

We are thrust because of circumstances into the position of developing a homemade self that does not conform to reality. Everything entering into the world that makes survival and security, affection and esteem, and power and control our chief pursuits of happiness has to be judged on the basis of one question: Is it good for me? Hence, good and evil are judged not by their objective reality, but by the way we perceive them as fitting into our private universe or not...the homemade self or the false self, as it is usually called, is programmed for human misery.

The combination of...two forces—the drive for happiness in the form of security and survival, affection and esteem, and power and control, and over identification with the particular group to which we belong—greatly complicates our emotional programs for happiness. In our younger days, this development is normal. As adults, activity arising from such motivation is childish...Without facing...early childhood excesses and trying to dismantle or moderate them...they continue to exert enormous influence throughout life (Iachetta 2009, 58–59).

Welcoming Prayer is a tool to dismantle, process, and gain relief from the afflictive emotional energy and behaviors of the homemade self—the false self.

Mary Mrozowski, a close associate of Thomas Keating, was the founding genius of the Welcoming Prayer. Three significant factors in her life influenced her creation of the Welcome Prayer. The first influence was her captivation with the seventeenth-century spiritual classic Abandonment to Divine Providence by Pierre de Caussade. Through the grace of Caussade's contemplative wisdom, a deep interior attitude of surrender developed within Mary. The second influence was her friendship with Thomas Keating where she learned of his evolved teachings on the false self and the destructiveness of the false energy systems. She had a keen awareness of the necessity for dismantling the energy of the false self and she knew intuitively that only through surrendering to God was that possible. A third influence came to her through her work as an administrator at a psychiatric hospital where she learned the techniques and benefits of biofeedback. In 1980, she creatively integrated all three influences; her own interiority of surrender, Keating's work, and the concept of biofeedback to create the Welcome Prayer.

The Welcoming Prayer diverts the direction of emotional and physical energy seeking desperately to compensate for afflictive feelings and thoughts. There is a narrow window of opportunity, after we first begin to feel the stirrings of false energy, in which we must consciously change our direction; it is when the storm clouds are first seen on the horizon, when the frustration first begins to build and before the debilitating energy becomes overwhelming. Keating describes this window as a nanosecond and warns that we must be very astute or the reactivity of the unenlightened unconscious will carry us away. Sometimes, it may take a long while to recover from the wild storm that ensues.

The Welcoming Prayer is a three-step process that "essentially redirects the pathway of the energy through the body so that it is liberated from the false energy system and recaptured as vital energy for inner transformation" (Bourgeault 2013, 142).

Step 1: Focus and Sink In

To focus on the storm-energy within means to pay attention to where you are holding it in your body. Is your stomach tense or your breathing shallow? You may even be holding your breath for short periods. Perhaps your shoulder and neck area is tight, or your jaw clenched. If the energy is very strong, you may feel faint or, if extreme, you may faint.

Stay with the experience. Be totally present to it. Do not attempt to analyze or change it. Simply sink into it. Feel yourself drop down into it.

Do not try to repress it—repression will lead to disassociation that will cause further separation from your true self. Repression is counterproductive to growth on the spiritual path.

Focus on your body and its sensations and sink deeply into them.

Step 2: Welcome

This may seem very counterintuitive! What you really do not want, you are asked to welcome!

By welcoming the destabilizing feeling or thought, an atmosphere of hospitality is created. A welcoming attitude is far more life aligning than defensiveness. In welcoming we disarm the demon, and when he is disarmed we become calm and can respond with gentleness and compassion rather than the reactivity of fear or rage. We can return to clarity and make a conscious decision what we will say or do.

In regard to dealing with the dilemma of emotional upset, the teachings of the Buddhist monk and poet, Thich Nhat Hanh, echo those of the Welcome Prayer. He counsels us to be hospitable, to say, for instance, to our fear, "Hello, fear. Sit down and we'll have tea." So we are to have tea with our fear, anger, shame, and so on!

It is necessary to clarify what is to be welcomed. "What you are welcoming is the physical or psychological content of the moment only, not a general blanket condoning of a situation… For example you are not to welcome incest or cancer but rather the feeling the experience triggers for you: the fear or rage or shame…" (Bourgeault 2013, 146).

Step 3: Letting God

Do not rush into this step of the process. Stay with the focus and sinking in and with the welcoming until you begin to feel, in your body and heart, some dispersion of the energy. The storm clouds will gradually begin to dissolve and recede somewhat. When you sense the ease of the energy abating then you are ready to move into the final stage of the prayer, the letting go.

There are two ways to go about letting go. You can, for instance, simply say, "I let go of my anger." Or you can use the more complete way that Mary Mrozowski recommends. The first three statements address the three false self-centers as defined by Keating and in naming them, we send a strong message to the unconscious (Bourgeault 2013, 147). The last statement is the zinger. It is the pure surrender of the entire situation and removes it from the mentality of having to correct, change, or fix it.

I let go of my desire for security and survival. I let go of my desire for esteem and affection. I let go of my desire for power and control.

I let go of my desire to change the situation.

The letting go is not a final renunciation of the particular feeling or turmoil; it is more like a gentle good-bye, a farewell wave.

Our spiritual transformation toward fullness of life in Christ is all about our alignment with our truest self in God. It is our lifelong task. The German mystic Jacob Boehme described it:

Here now, is the right place for you to wrestle before the divine face. If you remain firm, if you do not bend, you shall see and perceive great wonders. You will discover how Christ will storm the hell in you and will break your beasts...
(Bourgeault 2013, 149)

Jesus speaks to us, "It's all right; I am here! Don't be afraid."

Appendix C

Spiritual Direction

One of the precious practices of our Christian tradition is spiritual direction.

The term "spiritual direction" seems to indicate the giving of direction to another. However, spiritual direction is a form of pastoral counseling that focuses, not in giving direction to another, but on a person's relationship with God. Spiritual direction is also variously called spiritual friendship or companioning.

Spiritual direction is not therapy, but it can be a source of healing. It is not teaching but often leads to meaningful learning. It is a time to speak one's truth to another, and as we are heard, we are better able to hear what we are saying, and what God is doing in our life.

The gifts of spiritual direction can be profound. Through the graced experience of spiritual direction, the directees are encouraged to look beyond the present moment to see how God has been actively involved in all the circumstances of their lives. They are assisted in their reflection on how the energy of loving relationships has moved them toward wholeness and how suffering, pain, and failure have served their growth toward greater consciousness and complexity. The directee's trust in a God of love is nurtured, and he or she is supported toward the vision of seeing oneself as having a particular role to play in the larger picture of the coming of the Kingdom.

REASONS FOR SEEKING SPIRITUAL DIRECTION

The occasion for seeking spiritual direction usually arises from an inner yearning for a deeper intimacy with God. This yearning may express itself as a desire to improve one's prayer practices; for instance, there may be a desire to explore different ways of praying such as focusing more on the use of scripture in prayer or learning the practice of centering prayer as well as varied other forms of prayer. One may feel called to embrace a particular spiritual practice such as the Spiritual Exercises of St. Ignatius, or one may have the desire to develop a more contemplative way of living. Spiritual direction may be sought as a help in more fully integrating one's faith life with the relationships within one's chosen vocational commitment: within marriage, family, or community or in one's work and friendships. At times, it may be a significant decision to be made, as in a vocation to be discerned. It may also be a problem to be solved, or an addiction to be encountered that prompts one to seek the discernment that direction offers.

DIRECTOR

The choice of a spiritual director is important, and it is advisable that the potential directee prays to find the person who can most support his or her spiritual journey. One will look for a director who is experienced in the life and practice of prayer and has had professional training in what is considered not only the science of spiritual direction but also the art of spiritual direction.

PRESUPPOSITIONS FOR A FRUITFUL EXPERIENCE OF DIRECTION

+ If spiritual direction is to be effective, a regular and disciplined prayer life is essential. Prayer is the integrating force in one's life and shapes our attitude toward God. It is through our prayer that God reveals God's own self to us.

+ The guiding framework of Christian life, a life flowing from prayer and reflection is discipleship, which is fostered in the knowledge of Christ, in the intimacy of relationship with Christ and a desire to respond to Christ in service.

+ A relationship of trustful openness between the director and directee is vital for the fullness of the Spirit's wisdom to emerge. Both individuals bear the responsibility to pray for and to foster this openness in their relationship.

SPIRITUAL DIRECTION SESSIONS

Prior to beginning of a spiritual direction relationship, the director and potential directee discuss and agree to certain terms such as the frequency of direction, the place of direction, the fee to be paid, or donation to be offered. The director assures the directee of confidentially and also informs the directee that he or she and the director will, after a specified period of time, prayerfully evaluate how their relationship has developed and if they both feel it is fruitful to continue.

Spiritual Direction sessions are typically conducted in a contemplative manner beginning and ending with prayer. The directee needs to prepare for the session by reflecting on the events of the period since the last direction session. What have been the joys, successes, struggles in prayer and outside the time of prayer? In the direction session, the directee shares the prayer of the past period: the regularity of prayer, the approach, the time, and the place. The director listens attentively, does not correct, but rather helps the directee to hear what she or he is saying. The director assists the directee in remembering what God, within the circumstances and events of their lives, has done for them and helps them to hear what God may now be asking of them. The director affirms the good perceived, encourages, and promotes it.

An ancient sage reminds us: "there is a polish for everything, and the polish for the heart is the remembrance of God."

Within the sacred relationship of spiritual director and directee, the heart, as the mirror of awareness, is polished and reflects the remembrance and image of God.

Appendix D

The Spiritual Exercises of St. Ignatius of Loyola

The Spiritual Exercises of St. Ignatius of Loyola are a month-long program of meditations, prayers, considerations, and contemplative practices that help Christian faith become more fully alive in the everyday life of contemporary people. It is set out in a manual that represents a formulation of the spirituality of Ignatius of Loyola. It is a series of prayer exercises designed to help a retreatant, with the aid of a spiritual director, to experience a deeper conversion into life with God in Christ.

These Exercises can be made in different ways: first, extended over approximately thirty days in a silent retreat away from home; second, as condensed into a weekend or an eight-day retreat based on Ignatian themes; third, in the midst of daily life, over a period of a number of months, usually from eight to nine months. This third way is also known as the "Nineteenth Annotation." In the Nineteenth Annotation of the Spiritual Exercises, the retreatant commits herself or himself to a daily hour of prayer, to changes in lifestyle needed to maximize the experience of prayer, and to meet weekly with a spiritual director.

The Spiritual Exercises of St. Ignatius of Loyola are a Christo-centric program of conversion, a concrete way of "putting on the mind and heart of Jesus." The exercises are divided into a preliminary Principle and Foundation, followed by four "weeks" or phases with accompanying prayer exercises for each week. The first week considers God's generosity and mercy and the complex reality of human sin; the second week focuses on the birth of Jesus, the early life and public ministry of Jesus, and the third and fourth on the passion and resurrection of Jesus. At the end of the experience of the Exercises, the retreatant is invited to choose a way of life that recapitulates the dynamic of the Exercises, in an exercise called the Contemplation for Divine Love.

Scripture passages are taken from the New Revised Standard Version (NRSV) of the Bible, 1898

Bibliography and References

Scripture

Anderson, Berhnard, with Stephen Bishop and Judith H. Newman. 2007. *Understanding the Old Testament*. 5th ed. Upper Saddles River, NJ: Pearson Prentice Hall.

Barti, Markus. 1967. *The Anchor Bible: Ephesians 1–3*. New York: Doubleday.

Berrigan, Daniel. 1996. *Isaiah*. Minneapolis, MN: Fortress Press.

Brown, Raymond. 1966. *The Anchor Bible: The Gospel According to John I XII*. New York: Doubleday and XIII–XXI, 1970.

———. 1970. *The Anchor Bible the Gospel According to John XIII–XXI*. New York: Doubleday.

Dahood, Mitchell. 1970. *The Anchor Bible: Psalms III*, 101–50. New York: Doubleday.

Fitzmeyer, Joseph A. 1981. *The Anchor Bible the Gospel According to Luke*. New York: Doubleday.

———. 1992. *The Anchor Bible: Romans*. New York: Doubleday.

Johnson, Luke Timothy. 1991. *Sacra Pagina: The Gospel of Luke*. Collegeville, MN: The Liturgical Press.

Lundbom, Jack R. 1999. *The Anchor Bible: Jeremiah, I–XX*. New York: Doubleday.

Munck, Johannes. 1967. *The Anchor Bible Acts of the Apostles*. New York: Doubleday.

Raviendra, Ravi. 2004. *The Gospel of John in the Light of Indian Mysticism*. Rochester, VT: Inner Traditions.

Reicke, Bo. 1964. *The Anchor Bible the Epistles of James, Peter and Jude*. New York: Doubleday.

Schneider, Sandra M. 2003. *Written That You May Believe*. New York: The Crossroad Publishing Co.

Wright, N. T. 2008. *Surprised by Hope*. New York: Harper One.

Ignatian Spirituality

Arrupe, Pedro. 1979. *Challenge to Religious Life Today*. St. Louis, MO: Institute of Jesuit Sources.

Barry, William A. 1994. *Allowing the Creator to Deal with the Creature*. New York: Paulist Press.

———. 2001. *Letting God Come Close*. Chicago: Loyola Press.

Bergan, Jacqueline Syrup, and Marie Schwan, CSJ. 1985. *Birth*. Winona, MN: ST. Mary's Press.

———. 1985. *Love*. Winona, MN: St. Mary's Press.

———. 1991. *Praying with Ignatius of Loyola*. Winona, MN: St. Mary's Press.

Bradley, H. C. 2002. *The 19th Annotation in 24 Weeks, for the 21st Century*. Philadelphia, PA: Saint Joseph's University Press.

Cowan, Marian, and John Carroll Futrell. 1993. *Companions in Grace*. Kansas City, MO: Sheed and Ward.

Cusson, Gilles. 1988. *Biblical Theology and the Spiritual Exercises*. St. Louis, MO: The Institute of Jesuit Sources.

———. 1989. *Spiritual Exercises Made in Everyday Life*. St. Louis, MO: The Institute of Jesuit Sources.

Daily, Brian E. 1995. "To Be More Like Christ." *Studies in the Spirituality of Jesuits* 27 (1)

1995. *Documents of the Thirty-Fourth General Congregation of the Society of Jesus*. St. Louis: The Institute of Jesuit Sources.

Dyckman, Kathering, Mary Garvin, and Elizabeth Liebert. 1989. *The Spiritual Exercises Reclaimed*. New York: Paulist Press.

English, John J. 1995. *Spiritual Freedom*. 2nd ed. Chicago: Loyola Press.

Fleming, David L. 1980. *The Spiritual Exercises of Saint Ignatius, a Literal Translation and a Contemporary Reading*. St. Louis, MO: The Institute of Jesuit Sources.

———. 1996. *Draw Me into Your Friendship*, 74. St. Louis, MO: Institute of Jesuit Sources.

———. 2004. *Like the Lightning*. St. Louis, MO: The Institute of Jesuit Sources, 2004.

——— 2005. *Discipleship and Its Foundations*. St. Louis, MO: Review for Religious.

Harter, Michael. 1993/2005. *Hearts on Fire*. Chicago: Loyola Press.

Ivans, Michael. 1998. *Understanding the Spiritual Exercises*. Trowbridge, Wiltshire: Cromwell Press.

Magana, Jose. 1974. *A Strategy for Liberation*. Jersey City, NJ: Program to Adapt the Spiritual Exercises.

Medaille, John Pierre. 1979. *Maxims of Perfection*. Erie, PA: McCarty Printing Corp.

Meissner, W. W. 1992. *Ignatius of Loyola, the Psychology of a Saint*. New Haven, CT and London: Yale University.

Merz, Eugene F., and Carol Ann Smith. 1996. *Moment by Moment*. Notre Dame, IN: Ave Maria Press.

Modras, Ronald. 2004. *Ignatian Humanism*. Chicago: Loyola Press.

Mossi, John P. 1996. "The Spirituality of Surrender." In *Contemporary Annotations*, edited by David L. Fleming, 166–72. St. Louis, MO: The Institute of Jesuit Resources.

Murphy, Charles C. 1981. "On Leaving Retreat; To Go out Can Be to Go In." In *Notes on The Spiritual Exercises of St. Ignatius of Loyola*, edited by David Fleming, 144–55. St. Louis, MO: Review for Religious.

Olin, John C. 1974. *The Autobiography of Saint Ignatius of Loyola*. New York: Harper, Torchbooks.

Peters, William A. M. 1980. *The Spiritual Exercises of St. Ignatius: Exposition and Interpretation*. Rome, Italy: Centrum Ignatianum Spiritualitatis.

Pousset, Edouard. 1980. *Life in Faith and Freedom*. St. Louis, MO: The Institute of Jesusit Sources.

Rahner, Karl. 1965. *Spiritual Exercises*. New York: Herder and Herder.

Savary, Louis M. 2009. "Ignatius's Contemplatio ad Amorem." *Review for Religious* 68 (3): 261–275.

Stanley, David M. 1967. *A Modern Scriptural Approach to the Spiritual Exercises*. Chicago: The Institute of Jesuit Sources.

———. 1986. *"I Encountered God!" The Spiritual Exercises with the Gospel of Saint John*. St. Louis, MO: The Institute of Jesuit Sources.

Traub, George. 2008. *An Ignatian Spirituality Reader*. Chicago: Loyola Press.

Veltri, John. 1998. *Orientations*. Vols. 1 and 2, Part B. Guelph, Ontario: Guelph Centre of Spirituality.

Young, William, Comp. 1959. *Letters of Ignatius of Loyola*. Chicago, IL: Loyola Press.

Contemplative Prayer

Bourgeault, Cynthia. 2004. *Centering Prayer and Inner Awakening*. Cambridge, MA: Cowley Publications.

Bruteau, Beatrice. 1997. *God's Ecstasy: The Creation of a Self-Creating World*. New York: Crossroad Publishing Co.

Frenette, David. 2012. *The Path of Centering Prayer: Deepening Your Experience of God*. Boulder, CO: Sounds True.

Iachetta, Stephanie, comp. 2009. *The Daily Reader for Contemplative Living: Excerpts from the Works of Father Thomas Keating*. New York: Continuum.

Johnston, William, ed. 1973. *The Cloud of Unknowing*. Garden City, NY: Image Books.

Keating, Thomas. 1997. *Open Mind, Open Heart: The Contemplative Dimension of the Gospel*. New York: Continuum.

———. 2008. *Spirituality, Contemplation and Transformation: Writings on Centering Prayer*. New York: Lantern Books.

Other

Abbot, Walter. 1966. *The Documents of Vatican II*. New York: America Press.

Alexander, Andrew. 1947. *Daily Reflection for Nov. 21, 2013, Creighton University Apostolic Fathers*. Vol.1. New York: CIMA.

Bonhoeffer, Dietrich. 1999. *Dietrich Bonhoeffer's Prison Poems*. Edited and translated by Edwin Robertson. Grand Rapids, MI: Zondervan.

Borg, Marcus J. 1994. *Meeting Jesus again for the First Time*. San Francisco: Harper.

Bourgeault, Cynthia. 2013. *The Holy Trinity and the Law of Three*. Boston: Shambhala.

Bruteau, Beatrice. 2002. *Radical Optimism*. Boulder, CO: Sentient Publishers.

Burke, Daniel. 2012. *Navigating the Interior Life*. Steubenville, Ohio, Emmaus Road.

Cannoto, Judy. 2006. *Radical Amazement*. Notre Dame, IN: Sorin Books.

Dear, John. 2007. *Transfiguration*. New York: Image Books.

Delio, Ilia. 2005. *The Humility of God*. Cincinnati, OH: St. Anthony Messenger.

———.2007. *Full of Love*. Cincinnati, OH: ST. Anthony Messenger Press.

———.2008. *Christ in Evolution*. Maryknoll, NY: Orbis Books.

———. 2011. *The Emergent Christ*. Maryknoll, NY: Orbis Books.

De Mello, Anthony. 1978. *Sadhana: A Way to God*. St. Louis, MO: Institute of Jesuit Sources.

Dupleix, Andre. 1999. *Fifteen Days of Prayer with Teilhard de Chardin*. Liguori, MO: Liguori Publications.

Eichner, S. M. Marura. 1953. "We Walk in Miracles." *America* 89 (13): 339.

Excerpt from "East Coker" from Four Quartets by T. S. Eliot. Copyright 1940 by T. S. Eliot. Copyright © renewed 1968 by

Esme Valerie Elliot. Reprinted with permission of Houghton Mifflin Harcourt Publishing Company. All rights reserved.

Faricy, Robert. 1981. *The Spirituality of Pierre Teilhard de Chardin.* Minneapolis, MN: Winston Press.

Francis, Pope. 2013. "A Big Heart Open to God." *Interview in America* 209 (8): 15–38.

———.2013. *Encyclical Letter: Lumen Fidei, the Light of Faith.* Vatican City

———.2013. *Apostolic Exhortation: Evangelii Gaudium, THE Joy of the Gospel.* Vatican City.

Gardner, W. H. 1953. *The Prose and Poetry of Gerard Manley Hopkins.* Baltimore, MD: Penguin Books.

Helminski, Kabir. 2002. *The Knowing Heart, a Sufi Path of Transformation.* Boston: Shambhala.

Hubbard, Barbara Marx. 2012. *Birth 2012 and Beyond.* San Rafael, CA: Shift Books.

Johnson, Elizabeth. "Deep Incarnation; Prepare for Astonishment." Lecture given Dominican University, Chicago, IL, Nov.?

———. 2007. *A Quest for the Living God.* New York: Continuum.

Karbon, Roger Vermalen. 2012. "Ordinary Times, Here and Now." NCR, August 2012, 2, Celebration publications.org.

Keating, Thomas. 2002. *The Transformation of Suffering*. New York: Lantern Books.

Laborintz, Rabbi Shoni. 1996. *Miraculous Living*. New York: A Fireside Book. Lakota Creation Myth, www.indianlegend.com/lakota.

Llull, Ramon. 1995. *The Book of Lover and the Beloved*. Translated by Mark D. Johnson. Warminster: Aris and Philips (Taken from Ilia Delio, OSF, Claire of Assisi: A Heart).

Lohfink, Gerard. 2012. *Jesus of Nazareth, What He Wanted, Who He Was*. Collegeville, MN: Liturgical Press.

MacLeish, J. B. 1960. *Best American Plays*. Edited by John Gasser. New York: Crown Publishers.

McCarthy, Cormac. 2006. *The Road*. New York: Vintage Books.

Merton, Thomas. 2003. *The New Seeds of Contemplation*. Boston: Shambhala.

Metz, Johannes B. 1968. *Poverty of Spirit*. New York: Paulist Press.

Needleman, Jacob. 2009. *Introduction to the Gurdjieff Work*. Sandpoint, ID: Morning Light Press.

Newell, Philip J. 2008. *Christ of the Celts*. San Francisco: Jossey-Bass.

O'Donohue, John. 1997. *Aram Cara*. New York: Harper Collins Publication.

THE USES OF SORROW from *Thirst* by Mary Oliver, published by Beacon Press, Boston Copyright © 2004 by Mary Oliver, used herewith by permission of the Charlotte Sheedy Literary Agency, Inc.

Pannikar, Raimon. 2004. *Christophany: The Fullness of Man*. Maryknoll, NY: Orbis Books.

Pearce, Joseph Chilton. 2010. *The Heart-Mind Matrix: How the Heart Can Teach the Mind New Ways to Think*. Rochester, Vermont: Park Street Press

Robinson, Edwin H. 1999. *Prison Poems*. Grand Rapids, MI: Zondervan.

Rohr, Richard. 2011. *Wondrous Encounters: Scripture for Lent*. Cincinnati, OH: St. Anthony Messenger Press.

―――. 2013. *Immortal Diamond*. San Francisco: Jossey-Bates.

Saint Exupery, Antoine. 1971. *The Little Prince*. Translated by Katherine Woods. New York: Harcourt Brace Jovanovich.

Sanchez, Patricia 2012. "A Universal Kiss." Preaching Resources, NCR, Mary 27, 2012, Celebration Publications.org.

Skehan, James W. 2001. *Praying with Teilhard De Chardin.* Winona, MN: St. Mary's Press.

Sardello, Robert. 2006,2008. *Silence: The Mystery of Wholeness.* Benson, North Carolina: Goldenstone Press

Stafford, William. "A Ritual to Read to Each Other" from *Ask Me: 100 Essential Poems.* Copyright © 1960, 2014 by William Stafford and The Estate of William Stafford. Reprinted with the permission of The Permissions Company, Inc. on behalf of Graywolf Press, Minneapolis, Minnesota, www.graywolfpress.1993.

———. "The Way It Is." from *The Way It Is: New & Selected Poems.* Copyright ©

1998 by William Stafford and The Estate of William Stafford. Reprinted with the permission of the Permissions Company, Inc. on behalf of Graywolf Press, Minneapolis, Minnesota, www. Graywolfpres.1993.

St. Symeon, The New Theologian from a Collection of Mystical Hymns.

Teilhard de Chardin, Pierre. 1960. *The Divine Milieu.* New York: Harper and Brothers.

———.1961. *The Making of a Mind.* New York: Harper and Row.

———. 1961. *Hymn of the Universe.* New York: Harper and Row.

Von le Fort, Gertrude. 1953. *Hymns to the Church.* New York: Sheed and Ward.

Waldron, Robert. 1999. *Poetry as Prayer: The Hound of Heaven.* Boston: Pauline Books and Media.

Wilder, Mary. 2013. "Voices of Harmony: Counsels from a Carmelite and an Ignatian Perspective." *Presence Magazine* 19 (2): 52–60.

About the Authors

Stepped in the Gospels through the lens of Ignatian spirituality, Jacqueline Syrup Bergan and Sister Marie Schwan have ministered separately and together for over thirty-eight years, beginning in northwestern Minnesota where they conducted days of prayer in the rural areas, established a Center for Christian Renewal, and eventually collaborated in the writing of the five-volume highly acclaimed Take and Receive series of books based on the Spiritual Exercises of St. Ignatius of Loyola. Throughout the years, they published several other books and materials related to Ignatian spirituality and became sought-after retreat directors. In May 2013, Jacqueline and Marie were recognized with the Hearts on Fire Writer's Award in Spirituality by the Loyola Institute, Los Angeles, CA.

Jacqueline Syrup Bergan, whose husband, Leonard Bergan, died in December 2015, is a mother and grandmother. She began her professional career as a nurse anesthetist and went from putting people to sleep to awakening them to the beauty of prayer and spirituality. Over the years she has lectured, taught Ignatian spirituality and Contemplative prayer, directed retreats and offered spiritual direction. Currently, she has a private spiritual direction practice and is associated with Sacred Ground Spirituality Center in St. Paul, Minnesota, as well as Spiritual Directors International. She makes her home on Bear Trap Lake in Wisconsin.

Marie Schwan, as a member of the Congregation of St. Joseph, has spent a number of years in post Vatican II and biblical renewal within her community and beyond, including fourteen years as associate director of the Jesuit Retreat House in Oshkosh, Wisconsin. For many years she taught in the summer sessions of the Christian Spirituality Program at Creighton University in Omaha as well as serving several years in ministry in the Diocese of Rapid City, SD, where she offered spiritual direction, conducted retreats, and was on staff for the Jesuit directed Commissioned Lay Ministry program and the diaconate formation program. Marie also served many leadership positions in her religious community.

This book, *Loved and Loving: Contemplation to Attain God's Love*, was completed under the mantel of love, gratitude, and grief. As they strived to finish this work, Jacqueline and Marie were aware of Marie's approaching death. This guide to prayer represents the conclusion of their thirty-eight years of working together to bring their love of Ignatian spirituality to the people of God. The great desire that energized their ministry was to set people's hearts on fire with the awareness of how much God loved them; to instill within the community of faith the image of a God of loving kindness, ever faithful, ever forgiving, ever present.

About the Artist

Rochester's art arises from his deeply contemplative nature and his inner alignment with the natural word. The exquisite sensitivity of his art stirs the innate spirituality within our hearts and graces us with a keen consciousness of the beauty of creation. His work evokes tenderness and joyful delight while, at the same time, departing to our yearning spirits a sense of comforting steadiness and inspiring hope.

He began his art career over thirty years ago, beginning with the mediums of silversmithing, pottery and music. His mother, Jacqueline Rochester, a prominent career artist, was a source of encouragement for her son, Gregg, and was instrumental in his decision to pursue a future in oil painting. Having, also, had a grandfather who was an artist, Rochester, no doubt, was endowed with genetic favorability. However, realizing the need for expansion of his natural talent, he earnestly pursued training and study. He received fine art training at the Instituto Allende, the Belles Artes (San Miguel de Allende, Mexico), and Dakota Wesleyan University. He pursued graduate level fine art study at Indiana University and Kansas University. His most recent painting studies were with renowned Utah tonalist painter, Michael Workman, at the Scottsdale Artist's School It was not long before Gregg Rochester closed his thriving practice of clinical psychology and fully embraced his new life and career as Gregg Rochester, artist.

Inspired by his love of the American Midwestern and Southwestern countryside, he began creating landscapes and animal studies. He enjoys working in larger formats, producing some works of mural size. Another source of inspiration for Rochester has been his love of bicycling. During the last few years, this inspiration has been given expression in a surprisingly unique manner. Through theme-orientated brush painting of bicycles, together with landscape paintings which suggest the view of the countryside from the cyclist's perspective, Rochester has gained a sure following of admirers. His show, featuring these bicycles and related paintings, is titled, "Le Tour d'Art", and has been enthusiastically received in exhibits throughout the United States. Rochester originally conceived of his painted bicycles as sculptural pieces, however, painted as they are on carbon bicycles by Hed Cycling, they frequently are taken off the wall and proudly ridden. Rochester enjoys being occasionally referred to as the "Bike Guy".

Rochester has enjoyed gallery representations in New York City; Scottsdale and Tucson, Arizona; Santa Fe and Taos, New Mexico; Chicago, Illinois; Colorado Springs, Colorado; San Francisco, California; Minneapolis, Minnesota; St. Louis, Missouri; Lexington, Kentucky; and Indianapolis, Indiana. He has been featured in shows in New York, Scottsdale, Taos, Colorado Springs, Minneapolis and other Midwestern venues.

Rochester has been named a "featured artist' on the National Endowment for the Arts website. Articles and descriptions of his work have been issued in several national art and design periodicals, including Art in America, American Artist, Southwest Art, Phoenix Home and Garden, Scottsdale Lifestyle, and Better Home and Gardens.

His paintings can be found in institutional, private, and corporate collections throughout the United States, Canada, Europe, and Asia. Rochester's painting, *Are We There Yet*, was chosen for public display in the Senator George McGovern Library and Center for Leadership. He was named "Wisconsin Artist of the Year" by TOSCA (Theater, Opera, Shakespeare, Culture, and Arts) a Minneapolis publication. He was commissioned by the Minneapolis Institute of Art, a major art museum in the United States, to paint a bicycle for the "Italian Fashion from 1945-Present" show. Rochester's art is frequently found in healthcare centers throughout United States and has been credited with imparting a calming and healing effect on both patients and staff.

Gregg Rochester is an artist for our times. His inspirited art of light, joy, color, and promise challenges the collective paradigm of chaotic fear, and darkness that pervades our global culture. Rochester's nurturing art encourages and raises our consciousness toward the restorative resonance that serves to empower our entry into the new paradigm of loved and loving.

www.greggrochesterart.homestead.com

Praise for Loved and Loving

A reading by Andy Alexander, S.J.,
The Director of the Collaborative Ministry Office, Creighton University

I loved receiving and reading this book. I was disposed to like this work, because I have so appreciated the previous works of these two women. The *Take and Receive* series is a spiritual classic. It is on the bookshelf in nearly every retreat house and spiritual director's office. Jackie and Marie have a "brand," a style of spiritual writing which is known for being reliably grounded in Ignatian spirituality and for being very accessible.

They are women of prayer with deep relationships with our Lord and it flows beautifully through their writing.

When, however, I saw the title and first thumbed through the index, I was surprised. I thought, "Nobody begins a retreat book with the last exercise of the *Spiritual Exercises of St. Ignatius of Loyola*, do they?" As I read through the book, I discovered the wonderfully brilliant insight which Jackie and Marie bring to us.

In this rich work, the *Contemplatio* of the Excercises becomes the lens through which we look back and experience the power of the Exercises. This set of reflections and exercises does with everyday life what Ignatius does with his retreat. The authors so understand the Exercises that they can take the final exercise of the retreat and take us into it profoundly.

The structure of this book makes it a rich "school of prayer," which the Spiritual Exercises themselves are. The introductory material on prayer and the final appendices are the kind of wise and practical guidance which many expect from these two spiritual writers.

The outline of the book itself is the text-the points-of the *Contemplatio*. Each part of the meditation is an opportunity to guide a person's appreciation of that point through the means of wonderfully written commentaries, rich with a variety of scriptural resources and the wisdom of a wide variety of spiritual writers. Each commentary prepares the way for a beautifully guided prayer. The prayer brings us, again and again, into the heart of this meditation: we are asking for the grace to be grateful. Ignatius uses the same phrase he uses at other key moments in the Exercises. We are asking for an "interior knowledge." It is something deep, experiential and felt personally. And, it leads, as he says, to response, to action.

I got the feeling, exploring many of the rich commentaries, and then the prayer experiences, that this journey of *Loved and Loving* would take an ordinary person deeply into the graces Ignatius is hoping for-the response, based upon profound freedom, of a person moved by love. Psalm 116 captures it for me: "What return can I make to the Lord for all his goodness to me?"

There is a design to Ignatius' *Contemplatio* and these authors understand it and follow it carefully. Ignatius desires for the person making a retreat to experience God's love, but to deepen that experience by recalling it, remembering and collecting how much it is, how personal it is. God's love comes through the memories of graces received, of course, but it is also seen in all of creation, and ultimately in a powerful image of God's love flowing, cascading down upon us like a waterfall.

Throughout the Exercises, Ignatius guides the one making the retreat to respond. This final exercise leads to a big response- the offering of oneself in the prayer he offers, "Take Lord and Receive." I imagined that the authors intended the reader to experience a growing desire to respond, with deeper gratitude and deeper joy, with deeper freedom and generosity.

Ultimately, Ignatius' Exercises help people become "Contemplatives in Action," in everyday life. *Loved and Loving* seems to me to be a quite wonderful means to help in that very Ignatian spiritual tradition. And, it does it easily. Anyone can pick this up and be opened to these Ignatian graces.

I think *Loved and Loving* is particularly relevant for our time because of the gift of Pope Francis for our world. Francis' message is resonating with people around the world. It is basically the message of the Gospel, and for those of us who know the

Spiritual Exercises, Francis' message is right out of the Exercises. *Loved and Loving* seems to me to be an apt companion for those desiring the "evangelical joy" Francis says we need so much. This work is a reflection and exercise in pray book form to lead one to the "Joy of the Gospel" in everyday life. The journey a person would make through these commentaries and exercises would lead to a profound joy and gratitude, which must express itself in response, in love.

I think Ignatius and Francis would delight in *Loved and Loving*, for the same reasons I do.

A statement of praise for *Loved and Loving* from Eugene F. Merz, SJ, award winning Ignatian author and renowned international retreat director.

If you liked *Babette's Feast*, you will enjoy *Loved and Loving* by Jacqueline Syrup Bergan and Marie Schwan, CSJ. You will feast on a rich, nourishing five course dinner based on Contemplation to Attain God's Love, the famous, crowning moment in The Spiritual Exercises of St. Ignatius of Loyola. You will dine with theologians like Ilia Delio, OSF, Elizabeth Johnson, CSJ, Teilhard de Chardin, SJ; with Pulitzer prize novelists and poets such as Cormac McCarthy and Gerard Manley Hopkins, SJ. The menu is rich in options, possibilities, invitations, resources, and practical suggestions—a very creative work of love about love!

Praise from Marie's sisters:
Sr. Pat Bergen, C.S.J.,
Leadership Team of the Congregation of St. Joseph

We, the Congregation of St. Joseph, missioned to "unity" through loving are honored to endorse *Loved and Loving: Contemplation to Attain God's Love,* co-authored by Jacqueline Syrup Bergan and Marie Schwan, C.S.J. Marie, a very beloved member of our congregation, did not live long enough to see this book come to print. However, she spent her adult life mentoring us and so many others in the art of living in love. Her presence spoke love and evoked loving. Marie's depth of spirituality and expertise in leading others is revealed on every page of this book. She and Jackie previously authored, among several other books on Ignatian spirituality, the acclaimed five volume *Take and Receive* series which make the *Spiritual Exercises of St. Ignatius of Loyola* available to everyone. Now they have taken their talent one more step in inviting us to live the fourth week of the Exercises in our daily life. For those who long to have their lives magnify love, for retreat facilitators, spiritual directors, and prayer companions who long to help others in contemplating love in daily life, this book is a treasure. Through *Loved and Loving*, Marie and Jackie continue their beloved ministry of leading all of us to the very heart of God, who is Love!